101 Secrets of Highly Effective Speakers

Controlling Fear, Commanding Attention

Second Edition

Caryl Rae Krannich, Ph.D.

IMPACT PUBLICATIONS
Manassas Park, Virginia

Second Edition

Library of Congress Cataloguing-in-Publication Data

Krannich, Caryl Rae
    101 secrets of highly effective speakers: controlling fear,
  commanding attention / Caryl Rae Krannich
        p. cm.
    Includes bibliographical references and index.
    ISBN 1-57023-178-8
    1. Public speaking. I. Title: One hundred one secrets of highly
effective speakers. II. Title: One hundred and one secrets of highly
effective speakers. III. Title.

PN4121 .K94 2002
805.5'1–dc21   2001051706

Publisher: For information on Impact Publications, including current and forthcoming publications, authors, press kits, online bookstore, and submission requirements, visit our website: www.impactpublications.com.

Publicity/Rights: For information on publicity, author interviews, and subsidiary rights, contact the Media Relations Department: Tel. 703-361-7300, Fax 703-335-9486, or email: info@impactpublications.com.

Sales/Distribution: All bookstore sales are handled through Impact's trade distributor: National Book Network, 15200 NBN Way, Blue Ridge Summit, PA 17214, Tel. 1-800-462-6420. All other sales and distribution inquiries should be directed to the publisher: Sales Department, IMPACT PUBLICATIONS, 9104 Manassas Drive, Suite N, Manassas Park, VA 20111-5211, Tel. 703-361-7300, Fax 703-335-9486, or email: info@impactpublications.com.

Contents

Command Attention—
Your Introduction Sets the Tone 57

Close With Power 76

Prepare Like a Pro 82

Control Fear 103

Dedicated to the many people in my life who mentored my accomplishments or encouraged their completion

- To my mother, Marjorie Woodring, who made education both important and possible.

- To my brother, David Woodring, who told me I would write this book.

- To my husband, Ronald Krannich, who convinced me I should write it.

- To my many teachers in the Kent Public Schools and professors at Mount Union College, The University of Hawaii, and The Pennsylvania State University, whose guidance enabled me to write it—too numerous to mention all, but a special tribute and thanks to:

Richard Roberts
Raymond Ford
Don Terry
Paul D. Holtzman
Kenneth D. Frandsen
Carroll C. Arnold

Introduction

CONFIDENCE AND PUBLIC SPEAKING ARE LIKE the chicken and the egg—the more public speaking you do, the more confident you become. The more confident you become, the more willing you are to make a speech. In the past 30 years, thousands of people—from college students, many of whom took a public speaking class only because it was a requirement for graduation, to adult professionals who wanted to gain the courage to give a speech—have passed through my classes and seminars on public speaking. Some came because they knew they needed to become more adept or more confident presenting their ideas to audiences. Others came because their boss signed them up and told them they had better be there!

At the beginning of each session I ask the participants to indicate what knowledge or skills they most want to take with them when they leave on the final day of class. By far the greatest need they express is to be able to control their apprehension about public speaking. Some people have put off taking the seminar for years because they did not feel they could get up and give a speech. A few had said "no" to promotions at work because the new job would call for them to present speeches. Most want to be able to organize their thoughts more coherently, present their ideas more clearly, and make dull material more interesting.

I've tried to put together a hands-on, reader-friendly book geared toward the person who needs to develop the skills to present a speech and gather the courage to actually do it! Each of the 101 "secrets" here, if followed in the order they appear, will take you through the process of putting together, practicing, and delivering a speech. Don't try to take short-cuts by skipping some steps; put each step into practice and you can be an effective speaker.

The book provides the information, but you have to put yourself into a position to give speeches and gain the experience. Reading about it is the start, but you have got to do it. Having successful experiences behind you and being prepared are the two most important keys to building your confidence.

The secrets will give you the roadmap; the destination and the route must come from you—the speaker. Speak from your heart about things you care passionately about. Speak with enthusiasm borne of that passion. Provide your listeners with examples, stories, comparisons, and, where applicable, statistics that will both lend credibility to your ideas and make them come alive as well.

Because I have authored several books on careers—interviewing and other job finding skills—and since I conduct the seminars on public speaking, before the first edition of this book was published, I was often asked why I had never written a book on public speaking. My answer was always the same. There were a lot of good books already out there on public speaking and I didn't know that I had enough new to offer.

Then a need began to take shape in my mind. There were books that offered good advice, but I had found few that took the reader step-by-step through the entire process of formulating, practicing, and delivering a successful speech. Many books focused on a few aspects of good or effective public speaking. Some seemed to provide the author a chance to share personal stories about working with or for famous people, but seemed to stop short of providing the "how to" for the individual who wanted to develop his own comfort level and competence to formulate and deliver a speech.

The focus in this book is on the skills to put together and deliver a good speech as well as an effective speech. Good + Effective = Successful.

Through much of the book "he" is the pronoun of choice. To use s/he or to keep switching back and forth from one to the other interferes with easy reading of the message. The use of "he" is only for ease of reading and in no way is to suggest that the skills discussed are a male domain. As a female, I am comfortable with this usage and assure you that many of the best speakers (and listeners) in my seminars are women!

Before You Begin

AN ADVERTISING EXECUTIVE PRESENTS THE NEW advertising campaign to Revlon; an architect unveils the plans for a new hospital wing in Salt Lake City; a contracting officer at the U.S. Department of Health and Human Services explains the request for proposals to a group of potential contractors in Washington, DC; a college president in San Francisco speaks to an alumni group appealing for financial support for the building expansion program; a parent gets behind the microphone at a PTA meeting in Ohio to protest the school board's plan to close her child's school.

Facing the #1 Fear

Every day thousands of people present speeches. Many people fear having to present a speech more than any other situation they encounter. Now this may not sound strange to you—

especially if you are scheduled to give a presentation soon and you are already feeling nervous as you anticipate the speech. However, would it surprise you to know that though public speaking is #1 on the list of people's fears, #6 on the list is the fear of death? So what is the worst thing that can happen to you? You approach the podium to deliver your speech with dread and fear mounting, and as you look out over the audience, you drop dead of fright. In an instant, you have dropped from the #1 fear to the #6 fear!

> ► *Success Tip*
>
> Fear of speaking before a group is very real—the #1 fear in most people's lives. But you can learn to actually enjoy giving a speech if you practice the secrets of highly effective speakers.

Yes, I do say this facetiously, but I hope you have at least cracked a smile. People's fears about speaking are very real; these fears are no joking matter if they have kept you awake nights worrying about presentations or kept you from accepting a promotion because you realized that with the new job and title would come increased assignments to make presentations. But if you can smile and relax a bit, perhaps you can be open to the possibility that it doesn't have to be that way. You can, with a little guidance and some positive experiences, actually enjoy the opportunity to share your ideas with an attentive audience—and attentive they will be if you practice the many "secrets" of successful speakers outlined in this book.

101 Secrets Revealed

The "secrets" that follow are arranged in sequence. If you are a novice, you may wish to start with #1 and move through each of the 101 secrets. Together they form a series of steps—from start to finish—that will guide you in succession through the preparation and delivery of an effective presentation. If you are an experienced speaker and just want to brush up on selected skills, review the listing of secrets found in the table of contents (pages v-ix) and refer to those areas you wish to polish.

Some of the 101 secrets will be new to you—advice you have not heard before. Other secrets will seem more familiar. You may faintly recall having read or heard something similar— perhaps in that introduction to public speaking course you took years ago and promptly forgot, or maybe you thought you could take short-cuts, skip some steps, and be just as effective! Perhaps you are a person like Jim, who prides himself on being glib:

> *"I don't need to prepare; I can get up in front of an audience and talk about anything."*

Then later at his annual performance appraisal, Jim hears from his boss that he just doesn't communicate coherently when he makes presentations. Or maybe like Ann, you spend a lot of time preparing your speech, but when you get up in front of the audience, everything flies out of your head and you are sure you appear to be a tongue-tied idiot. Whether your weakness results primarily from a lack of solid preparation, as does Jim's, or whether like Ann you concentrate on yourself—worrying about how you're doing to the point of forgetting everything else— **you can** become an effective speaker.

> ➤ *Caution!*
>
> "Winging it" before an audience is a good recipe for showcasing your weaknesses. While you may be impressed with your platform savvy, chances are others won't!

Some of the "secrets" may seem so obvious to you that you wonder why they are even listed as secrets. *"Doesn't everyone know that?"* you may ask. Over the last thirty years I have taught, coached, and cajoled thousands of people to become better speakers. Some wanted to learn to be effective speakers. Others had tried to avoid presenting speeches and came only because their boss sent them to the seminar.

Let me assure you that every "secret" shared here is in response to some speaker's real-life success or initial failure. Resolve to let none of the failures remain your failures! As we begin, let's look at some commonly held misconceptions about making presentations to audiences.

Common Myths of Making Presentations

What do you know about giving a speech? How do you start, what do you say, and how do you plan to finish? Most speakers organize themselves according to certain beliefs about how to best approach a group and give a speech. While some of their beliefs may be helpful, others may be a hindrance to effective speaking. Look at each of the following statements. Which ones do you consider "true" and which ones "false"?

1. Memorization is the key to effective presentations.   T   F

2. The more notes speakers bring with them to the podium, the more successful their their speeches will be.   T   F

3. Any feelings of nervousness are bad for the speaker.   T   F

4. Speakers should not gesture, as any gestures distract the audience.   T   F

5. Speakers need not look at the audience more than 50% of the time; they should focus most of their attention on their notes.   T   F

6. One of the best and most effective ways
   to begin a speech is to start with a joke.   T   F

7. If the speaker is one of several speakers on
   the program, each speaker need not know
   ahead of time what other speakers are going
   to say; it is best for the material of others
   to be new on the day of the speech.   T   F

8. A speaker may dress as he or she pleases
   as long as the speech is well prepared.   T   F

9. It is not a good idea to practice a speech;
   the material will sound more natural and
   fresh if the speaker has not gone through
   it ahead of time.   T   F

10. The best speaking is done "off the cuff"
    with little or no preparation.   T   F

If you responded with a resounding "false" to each of the above statements, you are starting with an understanding of some basic concepts. We will look at suggestions later for putting the concepts into practice. If you responded "true" to any statements, by the time you finish this book you should understand why "false" is a better response.

Your Presentation Comfort Quotient

How comfortable are you in giving a speech? Let's check your "presentation comfort quotient" to see what skills you may need to polish before we begin examining each secret.

The following statements express feelings which many people have about presenting a speech. How many of these feelings do you share? How strong are your feelings? Circle the number on the right that best corresponds to how you feel about each one. Be honest, since no one need see the score but you.

1 = Always or Almost Always   4 = Seldom
2 = Frequently   5 = Never
3 = Sometimes

1. I feel nervous when I am going to have
    to make a presentation to several people.   1   2   3   4   5

2. If I am in front of a group of people,
    I worry about how I am doing.   1   2   3   4   5

3. When I am giving a speech, I try to avoid
    making very much eye contact with my
    listeners.   1   2   3   4   5

4. When I am making a presentation, I feel
    that people really aren't listening to me.   1   2   3   4   5

5. I have trouble getting started. I don't
    know how to begin.   1   2   3   4   5

6. I have trouble organizing my ideas.   1   2   3   4   5

7. Even though I am anxious for my
    presentation to be over, I don't know
    how to finish.   1   2   3   4   5

8. I know I say "ah" and "and uh" too
    frequently.   1   2   3   4   5

9. I think I ramble and have trouble
    keeping focused.   1   2   3   4   5

10. I have trouble delivering bad news—
    what I know my listeners don't want
    to hear—in a speech.   1   2   3   4   5

                                   TOTAL   [   ]

Now add the numbers (each is between 1-5) you circled to get your presentation comfort quotient. A total score of 50 would indicate you are very self-assured and have few apprehensions about making presentations. If your score is 10, you really feel unsure of yourself and very apprehensive about giving a speech. However, it is unlikely your score falls at either end of these extremes. Most people, if they are honest with themselves, fall somewhere between.

If your total is score is 45 or higher, you probably don't need this book! If your score fell between 35 and 44, I predict you have assurance and skills that place you above the average. You may wish to read on to gain a few additional skills, but most of all to add polish to those you already have developed. If your total score was between 25 and 34, you are with the vast majority of the population. You can build on the strengths you already possess and strengthen those areas in which you may be weak. If your score fell between 10 and 24, you are a bit more apprehensive than most, but you are certainly not alone. You have lots of company. Work on both developing your skills and building your self-confidence. I will wager you come across to your listeners a lot more confident than you think you do.

Not all of the secrets that follow are exciting. Some are relatively easy to do and will take little time. Others are more difficult or time consuming. But each is important, and in most cases one will build upon another. Taken together, they form the steps each of us can take to move from timid to assured; from confusing to lucid; and from just filling time to commanding the attention of our listeners as we make presentations that are both good and effective.

Plan To Exceed Expectations

1. Prepare Early

In real estate the watch-words are "Location, Location, Location." In public speaking the watch-words are "Preparation, Preparation, Preparation."

Most of us tend to procrastinate—at least occasionally. It is so easy to put things off—especially those things we do not look forward to doing. So if a speaking engagement is several weeks off, we can rationalize that we still have plenty of time. But as the day draws closer, panic can soon set in. Don't let this happen to you. Start preparing as soon as you are given (or accept) a speaking assignment. You have much to do and to do it right will take time. How much better your speech will be and how much better you will feel if you have taken the time to do it right. Few things are as great a confidence builder as knowing you are prepared. When you are prepared, you have:

- gathered the needed data

- determined what is appropriate to the listeners' understanding and belief/acceptance levels, as well as what they need to know

- organized the ideas so they flow logically

- selected examples and other supports for your ideas that will help clarify your points and make them interesting to your listeners

- developed a great opening that you know will capture the attention of even the daydreamers in your audience

- developed two great closings for your speech that will leave your audience focused on the central theme of your message

- checked out the room where you will be speaking

- requested any feasible changes you wish in the set-up of the room

- "talked through" the speech several times to your spouse, a friend, or a clock

If you're prepared, you've done all these things plus many others we will look at as additional secrets unfold. But most of all, you are confident that you know—really know—the material you plan to share with your audience. You are familiar with it because you have spent so much time with it—selecting and organizing the ideas that will best convey your message to your listeners. Because you know the material so well, you are more confident that you can talk about it to the audience – naturally – using your notes.

If you have waited until a few days before your presentation to begin to prepare—or worse yet, the day before—no doubt you will be apprehensive and with good reason. The normal butterflies you feel at getting up to make a presentation are intensified by the realization that you are not well prepared and now there is not enough time to engage in more than a superficial attempt. "Winging it" will come across as just that. Both you and the audience will feel uncomfortable. Like retirement planning, it is never too early to start preparing for your presentation. So start preparing right away—as soon as you know you will be making a presentation. It is the first step toward becoming an effective speaker.

 Success Tip

Check out the room ahead of time to make sure it's set up properly. If you don't, you may be in for some unexpected surprises that may diminish your effectiveness.

2. Plan to Be Effective

Listen to what other members of the audience say as they leave the room following a speech—someone else's speech. Many will not be talking about the speech at all. They have already moved on to other concerns: a project that they will be working on that day or perhaps their plans for the weekend. If they do allude to the presentation, you are likely to overhear positive comments about how good it was or perhaps negative ones such as that it was hard to follow the ideas presented.

Boiled down to its essence, there are three possible out-comes to a presentation:

1. **It is irrelevant.** People attend; perhaps they listen or they may sit politely and only appear to listen; they leave and never give another thought to the message.

2. **It is evaluated as good—or poor.** As the audience members leave the room, they comment on what a good speech it was; or how poor it was. They enjoyed it; or they did not enjoy it. It was interesting; or it was boring.

3. **It is effective.** Now certainly you would be pleased—perhaps overjoyed—to hear what a great speaker your audience thought you were and how much they liked your presentation. Nothing wrong in that, in fact, I want you to be a good speaker. But if that's all there is, to paraphrase an old song line, you've come up short. I want for you more than just being **good**. You also need to plan to be **effective**.

To be effective means your message has created change in your listeners. Your message has added to their knowledge, or you have convinced them to believe or accept an idea, or you have persuaded them to act on something. If you present information, you have been effective when they understand a concept or a process better than before. If you attempt to convince listeners of something, then you are effective if they accept the point of view you present. If you want listeners to behave in a certain way—to do something, such as buckle up each time they get in a car, or to discontinue a behavior, such as to quit smoking—you are effective if they do what you have advocated.

What are your goals as a speaker? Here are possible goals and corresponding responses desired from listeners:

Speaker's Goal	Desired Listener Response
■ To Inform	■ Understanding
■ To Convince	■ Belief/Acceptance
■ To Actuate	■ Do the Behavior/Stop Behavior

If your goal was for listeners to understand the advantages versus disadvantages of the company's new health plan, and most of the audience leave your presentation with that understanding, your presentation was effective. If you want your audience to accept (believe) that the new health plan offers them better benefits than did the old company plan, do they now accept this? If they do, you were an effective speaker. If you want your listeners to stop smoking, do they? Or if you want them to "buckle up" every time they get in a car, do they? **You are an effective speaker if** your listeners understand the concept, accept the premise, or engage in the behavior you were promoting.

Perhaps the difference between what is meant by "good" versus "effective" was best summed up by Adlai Stevenson who observed, "When Cicero finished an oration, the people would say, *'How well he spoke.'* (A good speaker) But when Demosthenes finished speaking, the people would say, *'Let us march.'*" (An effective speaker) A good speech results from the speaker's selection, organization, and presentation of ideas. An attention-getting introduction; main points that are well supported, developed, and organized; a conclusion that provides a summary and then hits the listeners with a memorable impact statement; a delivery that is dynamic and easy to listen to—these are all elements that, if done well, result in a good speech. An effective speech results from the thorough analysis of the audience that allows the speaker to focus on the needs of **this** audience and to select ideas and supports that will be appropriate for **this particular audience**.

If you internalize the "secrets" throughout this book, you can become a speaker who is both good and effective. Good plus effective equals a successful speech. Your listeners will say *"How well he spoke,"* followed by *"Let us march!"*

3. Determine Your Goal

We all want to take short-cuts. If there is a faster or easier way, we try to find it. But in taking what we perceive to be short-cuts, we sometimes short-circuit the process instead. The result is that we actually spend more time than if we had done it right to begin with or we miss our goal entirely. You might think that asking you to determine your goal as an early part of your preparation process is overly simplistic and hardly a secret to effective speaking. If so, you have not heard some of the

 **Caution!**

Speakers lacking a clear focus and goal tend to confuse their audience and engage in "streams of consciousness."

speeches that I have heard, nor asked the presenters following the speech what their goal had been. Your jaw might drop if you were to watch these speakers hem and haw as they attempt to articulate a goal for the speech they **just presented**! I might add that I normally would not ask this question of a speaker unless I suspected his goal was as unclear to him as to the audience.

So the lack of a clear focus and goal in the speaker's mind results in confusion and lack of clarity in the message. These speeches often wind up being "a stream of consciousness"—a string of thoughts related to the topic of the speech and tied together one after another. What is lacking is a clear main idea, development of the idea, and any hint of how we, the listeners, might be changed by these ideas. We come away confused rather than informed, convinced, or ready for action. So take some time to determine your goal. It should not be simply to "fill time."

You **must** have a message you believe in; one you believe your listeners must hear; one you believe can make a difference in their lives. You may wish to provide information on the relative benefits of the various pension plans they may select from; you may wish to convince them a new type of dental filling is superior to amalgam fillings; or you may wish to sell them on the new advertising campaign you have developed. Your goal does not have to be earth shaking, but you need to have a goal in mind; you need to believe in it; and your listeners need to feel it is important to them. If you can finish the sentence, *"I want my listeners to . . . ,"* fairly concisely, you have a goal statement and you are ready to start planning your presentation. No matter how good your idea, if it doesn't get through or doesn't get sold, you have not been effective. Effective speakers have a clear goal before they begin other steps in speech preparation. Constantly refer back to your goal as you prepare. It will keep you on target.

4. Analyze the Audience

This step is frequently overlooked by speakers who try to short-cut the process. But effective speakers make the effort. Every communication situation involves four elements:

- speaker

- audience

- occasion/situation in which the communication occurs

- message itself

An analysis of the speaker, audience, and situation must be taken into consideration in order to know how to best formulate the message—in this case your speech. If a speech is to be given to several different audiences, and is to be its most effective, it should be modified somewhat to fit each audience. You can put together a "good" speech and give it over and over again to many different audiences and it will still be good. But it may be only an effective speech—that is, your listeners understand the message or do what you persuade them to do—for one of those audiences.

Let's watch as Laura, a government employee with EPA (Environmental Protection Agency) gets a speaking assignment.

Laura's supervisor calls her into her office one day. She tells Laura that she is assigning her a trip to Alaska to make a presentation to a group of avid environmentalists regarding EPA's effort to protect Alaska's waterways and shoreline. Laura accepts the assignment with mixed feelings. She looks forward to visiting Alaska, but is apprehensive about the speech she will give. However, Laura starts out right. Even though she has two months before her presentation, she starts to work right away. She analyzes her audience, the situation, and the perceptions she believes the listeners will hold of her. She recognizes that she will be viewed as a representative of EPA and that this audience holds somewhat negative views of her agency's efforts to protect their pristine environment. Thus she decides to spend time near the beginning of her speech building common ground with her audience. She anticipates as many of their objections as she can and builds her speech from areas of agreement to controversial areas she cannot ignore. In short, she does everything right: she prepares early and plans to be effective by analyzing the audience—which includes their perceptions of her as the speaker—and the situation.

The night before she is scheduled to fly to Alaska, and eventually to Valdez where she is to present her talk, she retires early in order to be rested for the day ahead. The next morning she is awakened to news that while she slept, an oil tanker went aground in Prince William Sound. As she listens she realizes that although the full extent of damage to the environment is not yet known, it is suspected that this may be the worst oil spill to date. As Laura sits on the plane winging her way to Alaska, she is already hard at work making revisions to her speech. Through events beyond her control, the situation has literally changed overnight. She must now prepare for listeners who will likely be much more hostile than they would have been just one day prior.

The analysis of each of the elements of the communication situation is an on-going process; each audience is different and events can change the situation by the hour.

As you analyze your expected audience, you should address the following considerations:

- How large is the audience?

- What will be the ages of your listeners?

- What is the male to female ratio in the audience?

- How much education do your listeners have?

- What do your listeners already know about your topic?

- What are your listeners' attitudes toward your topic? Your stance?

- How open to new ideas will your listeners be?

- What are the listeners' relationships to you, the speaker?

- What are the relationships of audience members to each other?

- What are the listeners' attitudes toward you?

- Do listeners have a choice in attending?

Not all of these questions are pertinent to every speech, and every consideration pertinent to your speech may not be listed here. Go through the list and concern yourself with those that are pertinent and add any additional areas you need to consider.

The size of the audience will determine the number of handouts for your audience. Also, many speakers find it helps to prepare themselves mentally for a particular size crowd. Listeners' ages often will be

 **Caution!**

Expect some listeners to raise questions about your credibility—unless you establish your credibility at the very beginning of your talk.

immaterial; however, if you appear youthful and will be speaking to an older crowd about retirement planning, you would be well advised to try to boost your credibility at the beginning of your talk. No matter how great a speaker, you will initially encounter an *"he looks young enough to be my grandson; what can he teach me"* attitude. Besides, if you expect a homogeneous group of a certain age bracket, you can tailor your examples to that age group. The male to female ratio of listeners won't make any difference to how you organize and support some topics, but can to others. The educational level of listeners helps you gauge style and language, whereas their information level will be your guide as to how basic you need to tailor your comments on the topic.

Understanding listeners' initial attitudes and receptiveness to your viewpoint will help you to both select your supports and organize your thoughts to lead them to your premise. The relationship of listeners to each other or to the speaker may influence how or whether they interact with each other as well as the speaker. Are listeners in attendance by choice? Audience members who are required to attend a session can be reluctant —even hostile—listeners. Effective speakers know and adapt their material to their audience.

5. *Consider the Situation*

Consider Tricia, who prepared her speech and arrived for her speaking engagement to find she was one of several speakers on the program that evening. It was bad enough that Tricia faced a "not-so-fresh" audience following two speakers that preceded her. Worse yet, the speaker just prior to her presented much of the same material Tricia was prepared to present in her speech. Or what about Ted, who arrived to give his speech armed with several carousels of slides and found that the electrical outlet was on the opposite side of the room and he had no extension cord. Who would want to have been Saleena, who talked for an hour to a group who expected no more than a twenty-minute presentation.

It is never too early to check out the setting in which you will be speaking. Not only can you prepare for the situation you will encounter, but if what you find is not to your liking, you may be able to change the set-up of the room or even change to another location if you identify the problem early enough. Things to check on that will help guide you as you prepare your speech include:

- What is the size and physical set-up of the room?

- If the room is very large, is there a microphone?

- Is there a lectern?

- Is the lectern on a raised platform or on a stage?

- What are the lighting choices? Is the entire room lit evenly, or will you be on a stage that is brightly lit while the audience sits with house lights dim?

- Where are electrical outlets located?

- What is the availability of audio-visual equipment?

- What distractions are there likely to be? Will there be noise from outside, across the hall, or the space on the other side of the room divider?

- Can the seating be arranged to suit your presentation?

- Can the room temperature be regulated?

Don't limit yourself to consideration of the elements suggested above. Think about speeches you have given in the past as well as speeches for which you have been in the audience. What changes to the physical setting might have had a positive impact on the outcome?

I recall meeting a friend, who is a trainer in Thailand, for lunch at the World Bank in Washington, DC, where she was attending a conference. I had never previously encountered Chalintorn outside Bangkok, where I jokingly say there are three seasons: hot, hotter, and hottest! I was used to seeing Chalintorn in professional, yet lightweight clothing. To meet her at the World Bank and see her dressed in what appeared to be a navy wool suit was a switch. So I asked her if she had gotten the suit expressly for her trip to cooler Washington. "No," she said, "this is a suit I wear when I conduct training seminars. I ask to have the air conditioner set so it is very cool in the room. That way the participants easily stay awake. I wear wool suits to keep myself warm!"

One of Chalintorn's goals was to keep her listeners awake, and although I am certain she did not have to rely on the cool room to do this, it certainly gave her an edge.

There are other factors to be aware of related to the situation—beyond elements of the physical setting:

- **The time of day:** Will the audience be fresh, tired, or anxious to meet the afternoon car pool?

- **Other speakers sharing podium:** If there are other speakers, will you be the first speaker, in the middle, or the last to present? What will be their focus and their points of view? You certainly will have a hard time keeping listeners' attention if you are repeating half of the prior speaker's talk. If a speaker's point of view is different than yours, you may wish to deal with the differences head on— provide the audience with the reasons your point of view is more acceptable.

- **Time limits:** What are the time limits? Always expect time limits. Even if not explicitly stated, they exist in the minds of your audience members. If you exceed them, your audience will head for the nearest mental exit. Effective speakers keep situational constraints in mind as they prepare.

6. Highlight Your Strengths
7. Minimize Your Weaknesses

You have determined what you can about your audience and the situation. Now it's time to take a hard look at yourself—the speaker—from the perspective of the listeners. How do these listeners perceive you? Even if they have never laid eyes on you before, they do have preconceived notions about you: about your expertise, your honesty, your position on the issue, your willingness to defend your position. These opinions may have been formed through media coverage of you or may be the result of mindless gossip. Their opinions may not be based in fact. But remember: **a person's perception of reality is reality to that person.** So to be an effective speaker you must step out of your own perspective and try to look at how the other person—your listener—perceives the situation. You must find where your listeners' heads are and begin there to enhance your strengths and minimize your weaknesses **as they will be perceived by the audience.**

> You will recall James Carville's reminder on the walls of the Democratic campaign headquarters during the 1992 election which read, "It's the economy, stupid!" Contrary to popular belief, George Bush did not lose his 1992 reelection bid because of the actual state of the economy. The economy was already turning around—as

he claimed it was doing. But this took place in the late weeks of the campaign. People's perception of the economy was still rooted in a situation that no longer was valid. The President's situation was made worse by the fact that in earlier months, when the economy was in the doldrums, he would never admit there was a problem economy. So when the economy turned up, he no longer had the credibility on the issue to persuade the majority of voters that the economic upturn had already arrived.

It was poor communication, not a poor economy, that defeated the first President Bush as he ran for his second term. If he had admitted the problem economy existed in the beginning, formulated public relations to show the public that he was working to turn it around, "leaked" to the press he was making a trip to Capitol Hill to persuade Congress that his budgets were not "dead on arrival," he might have made a convincing case to the voters in the weeks prior to the election that the worst was behind us and better times were upon us. Carville's sign should have read, "It's poorly managed communication, stupid."

Though it is easier said than done, put aside your own frame of reference and try to look at how the audience members perceive you, the organization, or the point of view you represent.

For example, do you look young, but have a lot of experience? Attire yourself to look professional, speak with authority, and allude to your strongest related accomplishments. I recall a young woman in attendance at one of my seminars. She shared with the rest of the participants that her boss had sent her because she just didn't come across with authority when she made presentations. Some obvious things acting against her were:

- She was petite.

- She was youthful in appearance.

- She was dressed casually and youthfully.

- She hardly made eye contact with the audience— looking mostly at the lectern.

- She did not project her voice and even in a small room we had to strain to hear her.

- She spoke with excessive "ahs" which made her seem tentative and unsure of herself.

- She stood teetering back and forth behind the lectern.

- Her shoulders were hunched forward and inward and her body screamed submission.

What things can she modify and what can she not change? She will remain petite and, for now, young. These attributes are givens. But she can dress to give herself a look of authority, professionalism, and competence that will take the edge off her youth. She learned to look at her audience and engage each of them as her eyes scanned the room.

 **Success Tip**

You can shape the audience's perceptions of you and your message by the way you dress, stand, project your voice, and speak with authority.

When she projected her voice, not only could we hear her more easily and hence paid better attention, but she sounded authoritative and hence more credible as well. She came across as more confident as she lessened the number of vocalized pauses. She learned to plant her weight evenly on both feet and stand behind the lectern, pulling herself up as tall as her height would permit. She alluded to her experience where appropriate. When she left the seminar, she was well on her way to appearing much more confident and competent when she spoke.

Consider how your audience will perceive you and work to modify, where you can, those things that will enhance your presentation and further the progress toward your goal.

8. *Sleuth the Rest of the Program*

With what and whom will you be sharing the program? Is there a business meeting after which you are the featured speaker? Are there other speakers? Find out how long the other parts of the program are scheduled to take as well as the time limits placed on you. Don't let anyone tell you "take as much time as you need." There is no such thing; your audience will have expectations based on previous sessions. If you exceed the time expected, your listeners will take a mental exit.

 **▶ *Caution!***

Don't believe anyone who tells you to "take as much time as you need." Take lots of your audience's time and they will take a mental exit!

If there are other speakers, try to talk with each one prior to finalizing your speech. What are the others' focus; their stand on any issues; how long will each speak. What is the speaking order? If you are the final speaker (of several) for the evening, expect that you will be late getting started. Most of the previous speakers will have run over their allotted time and before you even begin, your audience is tired and some of your allotted time has already been taken. Plan ahead of time to limit the length of your remarks—your audience will be grateful and more attentive—and try to inject a bit of humor as you begin—assuming it is appropriate to the situation.

You're familiar with the expression, *"If anything can go wrong, it probably will."* Effective speakers try to anticipate what could go wrong and prepare contingency plans!

Build Your Body—Your Speech Body

9. Gather Information

Where do you start? Assuming that you are an "expert" on the subject of your speech—and this is why you've been selected or have volunteered to speak on this topic—you'll find that you have much of the information you'll use in your head. Start there. Because this is an area with which you are familiar, you will probably know individuals who also have expertise related to your topic. You may wish to contact some of them for more up-to-date or specialized information. Of course there are also printed materials that you will be familiar with or that the sources you contact will point you toward.

Don't overlook the people resources in your networks and use them when they can be helpful. As many of us went through school, research usually meant a trip to the library. To today's students it may mean a trip through cyberspace. But as you have established your career you have become an expert and have personal contacts who also have expertise. Printed data that is available at your office, local library, or on the World Wide Web are fine. Use them. But don't overlook what is often your richest source of information—your personal contacts.

10. Limit Your Time

You are sitting in the audience listening to a speech. Your expectation was that this would take about 15-20 minutes of your time. Mentally this time frame is what you are prepared for. However, the speaker has been droning on for over 40 minutes and shows no sign that he is about to conclude. As you look around you can tell that the rest of the audience is as uncomfortable as you. Their body language says it all.

What do you do? Do you get up and leave the room? Probably not—even though you might like

▶ *Success Tip*

Try to limit yourself to 20 minutes, the time the average adult can remain attentive to a speaker.

to. Most of us will stay even if it is a supreme test of our endurance. We won't physically leave the room, but we will take a mental exit. Our body remains, but our mind has left.

Studies conducted by social psychologists show that 20 minutes is the maximum time the average adult can remain attentive to a speaker. The admonition to speakers over the ages has been, *"Leave your audience wanting more."* Not bad advice, though perhaps easier said than done. Determine your listeners' time limits and resolve to finish sooner rather than later. No matter how important, no matter how voluminous your information, conclude well within the expected time limits.

After all, what your listeners don't hear has no impact on them. If they have taken a mental exit, they will not hear your message—no matter how important. Limit your time to 20 minutes if you can; more than double that time and your listeners will surely take a mental exit. Ask the program chairperson or someone familiar with the situation how long the program is expected to be. If you are speaking for a more lengthy session, make sure to give your listeners short breaks. They will come back more alert and able to listen more attentively. Effective speakers do not impose themselves on the minds of their listeners for longer than the posterior can bear!

11. Limit Your Focus

The secret to limiting your time is to limit your focus. Of course it would be difficult to share with your audience everything you know about a topic in limited time. But then they don't want to hear everything you know and it would most likely turn out to be a rambling stream of consciousness anyway! Remember Secret #3, "Determine Your Goal"? If you have concisely stated your goal you have taken the first step to limiting your focus. If you have followed Secret #4 and "Analyzed Your Audience" you have further limited your focus by determining what your listeners will need to hear. Consider time constraints as you determine your main points and develop your ideas. At this point you may further limit your focus if necessary to fit into the time available.

12. Develop the Speech Body First

Most speeches consist of three parts:

- introduction

- body

- conclusion

In simplest terms the **introduction** should gain your listeners' attention and orient them to the focus of your speech; the **body**—sometimes referred to as the "discussion section"—sets forth the main ideas and develops or supports the main ideas of your speech; the **conclusion** briefly reviews the main ideas and imparts a statement of impact—a memorable statement that focuses listeners' attention on something you want them to remember. You will deliver the parts in that order: introduction, body, and conclusion. But don't prepare them in that order. One of the fastest ways to develop "speech-writer's block" is to begin by preparing your introduction.

 *Caution!*

If you begin by preparing the introduction, chances are you'll quickly develop "speech-writer's block."

Begin by preparing the body of your speech. The body is the heart of your speech—the main ideas and their development. It will be easier for you to prepare the speech body first. Once you finish preparing the body you will know exactly what the speech message is. At this point you can move on to consider how to best begin your speech. The introduction should grab your listeners' attention and lead them to the ideas presented in the body of the speech. The conclusion will refocus your listeners on the main ideas you presented and then leave them with a statement of impact that will stick in their memory.

13. Determine Your Main Points

Once you have followed the advice in Secret #3—"Determine Your Goal"—you have a specific idea what you want your listeners to understand, believe, or do, after they have heard your speech. As you completed the task suggested in Secret #4—"Analyze the Audience"—you focused on specific attributes of your listeners as they relate to the topic of your speech, the setting of the presentation, and you, the speaker. Put together the information you have from following Secrets #3 and #4 and you should be able to articulate your main points. What do your listeners need, to move from where they are now (as revealed by your audience analysis) to where you want them to be (your goal statement)?

What your listeners need—either to understand your message or be persuaded—should determine your main points. Each main point should help move your listeners toward your goal. Focus is important. Don't let yourself get waylaid going off on tangents. A history of your subject may sometimes be germane to your goal, but most often it is extraneous. Remember you are not "filling time"; you are attempting to help your listeners move from one point to another. Each main idea should support this goal. After bounty hunters burst into the wrong house and killed two innocent people in Arizona, a speaker selected this goal and identified two main ideas:

> **Goal Statement:** To convince listeners that bounty hunters should be licensed; this would raise their competence and level of professionalism.

> I. In order to obtain a license to become a bounty hunter, the applicant must go thorough a background check for criminal history and mental stability.

II. In order to obtain a license to become a bounty hunter, the applicant must pass a test covering the laws that govern the identification of and apprehension of those who have skipped bail.

The most common mistake beginning speakers make is to select too many main points. You have limited time. You must limit the ideas you present. Three main points are plenty for most speeches. Each one of the main points must be developed with supporting materials, and to develop your ideas fully will take time.

Take, for example, a ten-minute speech in which you plan to present three main points. If you spend 1 minute each on your introduction and conclusion, you only have just over 2½ minutes to develop each of your three points. That is bare bones. Those bones need flesh, and developing that flesh—the subject of the next few secrets—takes time and a variety of supports such as quotations, statistics, examples, and comparisons to develop.

14. Use Supporting Materials Liberally: Build Credibility

Just because you make a statement, you can't expect that your listeners will accept it as fact, nor can you necessarily expect that they will understand it. Your main ideas must be amplified and supported in order to be understood or accepted. As you develop your main ideas, you help your listeners move from their present understanding or acceptance of your main thesis to where you hope they will be when you conclude your remarks. Supporting materials help a speaker:

- add interest . . . . listener is more attentive

- clarify a point . . . . listener better understands

- "prove" a point . . . . listener is more likely to accept

- make points memorable . . . . listener has better recall

- build credibility . . . . . listener is more likely to accept

Hence, the speaker's choice of supporting materials is made on the basis of his analysis of the audience. Obviously if my listeners are interested in what I say, they will be more attentive. That increased level of attention gives me a better opportunity to inform or persuade them. What will add interest for this audience? What do my listeners need to understand or to accept my proposition? How can I make the ideas I present truly memorable? The following nine secrets present the most frequently used forms and methods for supporting your main ideas in the body of a speech. Effective speakers enhance their ideas and build their credibility by using a variety of supporting materials, and they use supporting materials liberally.

15. Use Quotations/Testimony

If someone has said what you want to say better than you ever could, use quotations to support a main idea in your talk. Go ahead and use the great way someone else made the point, but give credit to the source so you will not be accused of plagiarism. Or you may choose to use a quotation because you believe the source itself will be a highly credible one to this audience, adding weight to the ideas you present.

Sources may be individuals such as a prominent scientist. A

source could be a formal group of people such as the AMA (American Medical Association). A source could be a publication such as *The New England Journal of Medicine*. You may have several sources available to you for essentially the same information, and you must select the ones you will credit. Your audience analysis should help you choose. As you cite the results of an extended medical study, you may have choices. Do you give credit by citing the researcher by name or do you credit *The New England Journal of Medicine* where the research results were published? To a group of laymen with no knowledge of the medical research community, you would probably allude to the published results and the journal, knowing that even people with no medical training have heard of it and know it is held in high regard:

> "According to the results of the study published in the May edition of . . . "

However, for a speech directed at persons in the medical community who would be familiar with the name and work of an eminent scientist, you would probably want to cite the researcher by name:

> "According to Dr. Franz Bonesetter and his study of . . . "

Of course, you could decide to attribute both the researcher and the journal for yet another audience:

> "The results of this study conducted by Dr. Ida Felbetter and published in the May issue of the *New England Journal of Medicine* . . . "

High credibility sources can be drawn from all sectors of society according to the topic under discussion as well as the views of the audience. You might not think at first that a convicted "cat burglar" would be a high credibility source. But who better as a source for a speech on how to safeguard your house against break-in and theft?

When presenting quotations, it is not necessary to preface with "quote" and follow it with "unquote." It is much smoother to indicate a quote to the audience by prefacing it with some variation of "According to . . .," " or following the quote with "Those were the words of . . . ."

Although many speakers build collections of quotations as they come across items that they believe they might use in the future, you will probably find plenty of material for use as quotations as you do research for your speech. There are also books of quotations available in your library as well as bookstores. However, these are likely to be filled with platitudes that are fine for a general speech but may not meet your needs on specific topics.

Quotations add authority to your speech, show that there are others—many of them experts—who share your point of view, as well as add interest and make points memorable.

16. Use Statistics

Numbers can be useful to:

- clarify an idea

- make an idea more meaningful

- communicate information more precisely

- present information more powerfully, believably, and hence more convincingly

Technically not all figures are statistics, but a technical distinction is not necessary in order to use numbers to advance and strengthen a speaker's ideas.

But numbers by themselves don't necessarily clarify. If you talk about "an area of 6,000 square miles," what meaning will this have to the average listener? But if you compare this figure to something more familiar to the audience, your support can add both precision and clarity. Consider a student at Penn State who, in a talk about his home country, Kuwait, made the following statement:

> "Ku   t is a small country in size. In fact, Kuwait is
> ma   up of only 6,000 square miles—that's about the
> siz   f Rhode Island and Connecticut combined."

By comparing the number of square miles with the area of two states his listeners were familiar with, he made the size of Kuwait much more meaningful to his audience. I might add that I originally heard this speech 25 years ago. I could not have even come close to citing the number of square miles without referring to reference material, but I recall to this day the speaker's comparison to Rhode Island and Connecticut.

Consider the following comparison by Richard Carrington, a science writer, who tried to clarify the immense age of the earth as well as the recent entry of man:

> "If the earth's history could be compressed into a single
> year, the first eight months would be completely with-
> out life, the next two would see only the primitive
> creatures, mammals wouldn't appear until the second
> week in December, and no *homo sapiens* until 11:45pm
> on December 31. The entire period of mans' written
> history would occupy the final 60 seconds before mid-
> night."

The following example shows how helping an audience to visualize what you are talking about can make an idea immensely powerful. Most of us, if asked the difference between a million and a trillion dollars, would be hard put to offer a good answer. We might jokingly say, "Give me either one!" or we might respond that a trillion has an additional six zeros. Look at the next quotation taken from President Reagan's speech made to a joint session of Congress about his first budget:

> "A few weeks ago I called such a figure—a trillion dollars—incomprehensible. I've been trying to think of a way to illustrate how big it really is. The best I could come up with is to say that a stack of $1,000 bills in your hand only four inches high would make you a millionaire. A trillion dollars would be stack of $1,000 bills seventy-six miles high."

I'll wager that most listeners, even members of Congress, were stunned. I certainly was. Granted, you don't have access to the speech writers of the President who will research and formulate impactful supports like Reagan's, but if you keep your goal in mind, know your audience, and think creatively, you, too, can formulate supports that will increase your effectiveness.

17. *Use Examples*

Examples, whether detailed illustrations or short specific instances, pique listeners' interest. An example may be actual or hypothetical. The following example of an actual situation is taken from a speech about the advantages of using a credit card to make purchases when traveling abroad:

"Another advantage of using your credit card for making purchases abroad is that if you find out later that the seller misrepresented the item you purchased, your credit card company may help you recover your money. For example, a few years ago a friend bought what was purported to be a ruby in a small border town in northern Thailand. She was told it was a nearly flawless ruby and thinking she was getting a deal, she paid $10,000 after hard bargaining. She charged it on her American Express card—you know, don't leave home without it! When she got home she had the ruby appraised and found out she had bought not a ruby, but a red spinel. It was worth a fraction of what she had paid. Though there was no requirement that they do so, American Express went to bat for her, and in the end brokered a deal in which Jo returned the 'ruby' and the shop credited her American Express card. A happy ending in this case. But if Jo had paid cash, she would have been stuck with a very expensive red spinel and a sour taste in her mouth."

Consider the following example in which the speaker tries to exhort the audience to imagine a situation most have never actually encountered:

"How can we understand what is happening in Bosnia? Many of us have never lived in a war zone. Oh yes, we hear about wars in far-off lands on the evening news. But most of us have not gone off to a distant land to fight a war, nor have we lived in a place where war was raging all around us. A place where when we go to bed at night we can't shut out the sounds of bombs falling, of sirens blaring, of shots fired, or of people screaming. We have not lived in a place where we wake in the morning and find our best friend's body laying face down in the street outside our door. The painful realities of war are impossible to imagine if our closest contact is the six o'clock news."

18. Tell Stories

Stories tell of events that have happened to people. Stories personalize a message, as listeners can identify with the people and the situations you relate. If you can relate an incident that actually happened to you and that furthers your goal to inform or persuade, that's a plus. If you can tell a story about a relative or a friend—that, too, seems personal because you are close to the source. Or a story may involve others whom the speaker has only read or heard about. But the audience can still relate to the real people and events involved. A recent seminar participant shared the following story from her life (along with numerous other examples) to support her belief that God talks to his people and those who know Him heed His voice:

> "My husband, Don, and I, try to hear Evangelist Tim Lee whenever he preaches within a 300-mile radius of our house. Dr. Lee's legs were blown off in a land mine explosion in Vietnam in 1971.
>
> In October 1996, Don and I went to hear Dr. Lee at a Baptist church in Alexandria, Virginia. We got to the service early because we had brought my mother with us and she uses a wheelchair. I noticed as soon as we got to the church that there were about 18 cement steps up to the sanctuary. We had to get someone to unlock the elevator to get my mother up to the sanctuary, and I noticed that he locked the elevator again as soon as my mother reached the foyer.

We were sitting in the sanctuary about 15 minutes before the service was supposed to start when I suddenly got the feeling that we should help Tim. I said to Don, 'Do you think Tim needs our help?' Don said, 'No, the minister has taken care of that.' I said, 'Of course; how silly of me.' The minister **always** made sure Tim had all the help he needed. Why would this time be any different?

About five minutes later I again got the feeling that Tim needed our help. I said, 'Why don't you check and see if Tim needs our help.' Don said, 'Paula, the minister has taken care of that.' About one minute later I felt very strongly that Tim needed our help. I could not leave my mother in the sanctuary by herself because she would start talking very loudly, so I said in a very determined voice, '**Don, go back and check**!' Don jumped up and almost ran to the foyer. He didn't come back for a long time. When he did come back, he said that the foyer was completely deserted when he got there, so he opened the front door of the church and looked down the cement steps. Tim was sitting at the bottom of the steps. As soon as he saw Don, he said, 'I'm so glad to see you. Can you help me?' Don said, 'I was **sent** to do just that.'

God could have told the minister that Tim needed help. I think he told me instead, because he knew Don and I would get a lot out of helping him that day."

19. Use Comparisons & Contrasts

Sometimes listeners can understand or accept a concept better if the speaker focuses on similarities or dissimilarities between things, concepts, processes, people, or places. A comparison presents characteristics, features, or qualities which are similar. It may show listeners a relationship between something familiar and something unfamiliar. It may show a relationship which is a surprise:

> "A recent televised Hollywood news clip mentioned that 'a motion picture was being filmed on a glacier near Juneau, Alaska. The Mendenhall Glacier's ice field covers an area larger than the state of Rhode Island'."

Comparing the size of the glacier to the area of Rhode Island made the magnitude of the glacier meaningful to an audience who had never seen a glacier.

A speaker in Virginia whose goal was to get listeners to fasten their seat belts used the following comparison as a support:

> "More than 15 million people are involved in traffic crashes each year. That's the equivalent to the population of New York City, Chicago, and the entire state of Virginia combined."

The number of people involved in crashes was made more significant for the audience by including the comparison. If combining more than one support helps makes the point clearer or more significant for your audience, use both. The speaker went on to say:

> "In 1990, three million people were injured and 42,000 died in auto accidents. That's an average of 115 deaths per day or the equivalent of a major airline crash every day of the year!"

Beth helped listeners focus on what it would be like to pick up the paper every day of the year and read that another airplane had crashed. The only difference is that the traffic accidents are dispersed across the country and do not get reported as an aggregate figure each day on the evening news.

Contrasts can be used to show differences between things, concepts, processes, people, or places. In the same speech focused on trying to get the audience to buckle their seat belts, Beth contrasted the cost in lives as well as money lost due to incidents of crime versus automobile accidents.

> "A murder occurs every 22 minutes; someone dies in an automobile crash every 14 minutes. An aggravated assault occurs every 30 seconds; someone is injured in a car crash every 11 seconds. Violent crimes cost society 14 billion dollars a year; traffic crashes cost society 74 billion dollars a year."

20. Demonstrate

Some ideas are made understandable by actually demonstrating how to do it or what it looks like. A speaker whose goal is to help listeners save lives by learning how to administer CPR on a victim who has stopped breathing, may explain the process. But he will certainly also choose to demonstrate how to administer CPR as a part of his speech.

21. Define Unfamiliar Terms

Your audience analysis should indicate whether you will be using words or acronyms unfamiliar to your audience. It's a good idea when using an acronym for the first time in a speech to follow it with an indication of what the letters stand for:

> "This morning I'll be discussing the new initiatives
> underway at DOT, the Department of Transportation,
> to promote the use of seat belts by drivers as well as all
> the passengers in their car—whether seated in the front
> or back seats."

From this point on, for most audiences, the speaker may use this acronym freely. It can become confusing if the speaker uses too many unfamiliar acronyms, as it is hard to remember what so many new terms stand for. Certainly there are acronyms that

> ➤ *Caution!*
>
> Be careful in using acronyms—
> some members of your audience
> may not be familiar with them.

have become so much a part of our vocabulary that listeners will know what they mean. The FBI or IRS, for example, probably do not need further explication to most American audiences. IBM is of such common usage that most people readily identify this company with, depending on their age, typewriters or computers. Many might have more difficulty with its full name—International Business Machines.

Definitions are especially useful when different meanings are possible or you are using a word in a different way than the norm. Operational definitions help you and your listeners stay focused on the way you will use certain words or phrases. What does a speaker mean by "gun control"? To one person it may mean taking gun ownership away from private citizens, while to another it may mean applying for a permit to own a gun with a five-day waiting period required between the application and the issuance of a permit for the purchase of a gun.

When I conduct public speaking seminars, I operationally define what different things we would look at when making a distinction regarding a "good" speech or an "effective" speech. We look at how "good" a speech was by examining the introduction:

- Was there an attempt to gain listeners' attention?

- Was the main focus of the speech apparent?

We would look at the body and ask whether the main ideas were well developed and organized logically. We would look at the conclusion and consider whether there was a summary as well as a concluding memorable statement. In determining whether it was an effective speech, we would ask whether the speaker's goal was achieved:

- Did the listeners understand? *or*

- Did they agree and accept? *or*

- Did they engage in the desired action/behavior?

If you believe many, but not all, listeners will be familiar with a term, it is possible to define the term for those who may be unfamiliar with it without offending those to whom it is common knowledge.

"Those of you from the DC Metropolitan area are of course only too familiar with our highways' HOV lanes. But for those of you joining us this morning from the regional offices, the HOV signs on our interstate highways here may be an anomaly. HOV is an acronym that stands for High Occupancy Vehicle and during rush hour periods only cars with three or more persons can legally drive in the HOV lanes."

Put this way, the local audience members who are familiar with HOV lanes will not feel the speaker is being condescending. Use your audience analysis to determine what terms, if any, may need defining. Effective speakers are considerate of their audience by defining terms or acronyms that may be unfamiliar to their listeners.

22. *Use Visual Aids Effectively*

Another method to enhance your presentation is to illustrate an idea. Visuals allow listeners to see as well as hear your message. As a method of support, visuals aid listeners' understanding and acceptance. Visual aids strengthen a speech in all the same ways as the other forms of support we have looked at thus far. Visuals help the speaker:

- Add interest

- Clarify a point

- "Prove" a point

- Emphasize a point

- Make ideas memorable

Visuals may be used as a method to emphasize a strong quotation, a significant statistic, an excellent example, a striking comparison, or an important definition. A demonstration itself becomes a visual. Visuals may be a few words written on a flip chart or a chalk board; ideas presented using an overhead projector; photos or slides to enhance your message; or state-of-the-art computer generated and interactive aids. The most commonly used visual media include:

- Handouts

- Flip charts

- Transparencies

- Slides

- Photographs

- Models

- Videos

- The thing itself

- Computer generated visuals such as Power Point

Success Tip

Visual aids can definitely enhance a presentation. But not every speech requires visual aids. Consider using them, but do so judiciously. Don't feel you always "have to" use them.

Not every speech needs a visual aid. Use visual aids only if they will enhance a presentation. The need for a visual should be apparent. If you are at a loss as to what visual to use, perhaps your speech does not need any. I recall talking with a reading specialist a few months ago. She had been asked to speak at her state reading conference. She was no doubt pleased at the invitation to speak, but she was especially proud of the fact that her speech was prepared and ready to deliver—two months prior to the conference. She rightly believed in preparing early! As she chatted with me about her talk, she confided that she had one problem. She had not yet decided what her visual aid should be. My best guess is that she did not need one. If she had finished her speech and did not yet have any idea what to use as a visual, one probably wasn't necessary.

If there is a visual that will help your audience understand your message, accept your premise, or act on your challenge— use it. If you can devise a visual that will keep your listeners' attention or help them recall your message later—use it. But there is no rule that says every speech must have a visual. The wrong visual can be a distraction and a detriment to a speech.

Visuals used properly can enhance your presentation, but using them effectively means observing certain rules or they can become a distraction.

Guidelines For Presentation of Visual Aids

1. **Show visuals only when you are talking about them.** If a visual is in view of your listeners before you refer to it or after you have finished talking about it, your audience will be distracted. You want your listeners to direct their attention toward you rather than the visual except when you are using it to make your point.

2. **Be certain visuals are of sufficient size and are placed so that everyone in the audience can see them.** If you select visuals that some listeners cannot see, no matter how great they are, you have lost the listeners who are unable to see them. They know they are missing out on something, and after straining to see and finding they cannot, they will give up and take a mental exit.

3. **Talk to your audience, not your visual.** Face your listeners and direct your comments to them. Glance at your visual briefly if you wish to point to it, but once you've found your place, focus your attention back on your audience.

4. **Be prepared for equipment breakdown if you are using mechanical or electrical equipment.** You recall Murphy's Law—if anything can go wrong it probably will. Anticipate what problems could occur and carry back-ups. Using anything electrical? Make sure you have an extension cord. Using an overhead projector? Go prepared with an extra back-up bulb. But what if the ultimate breakdown occurred? What if all electrical power were lost? Could you give the speech without the visuals if you had to? Anticipation of potential problems is one thing, but I do not encourage you to go so far as to carry an electrical generator with you. Use visuals to enhance your speech, but be prepared so that if it were necessary, you could deliver your presentation without them.

5. **Don't overdo.** The purpose of visuals is clarity and emphasis. If overused, everything and hence nothing becomes emphasized.

6. **Recognize that anything put in the hands of the listeners or passed around the audience is a distraction.** Anything put in your listeners' hands will focus their attention on it, and away from you. Consider carefully whether the information or emotional appeal the visuals add to your message will offset the distraction it will create.

A participant in my seminar a few years ago was an officer in the Norfolk Police Department. He was in charge of the division responsible for abused children. For one of his presentations, his goal was to actuate his listeners. If they ever seriously suspected a person of child abuse, he wanted them to report the situation to the authorities. He brought to his speech several sets of large glossy black and white photos of abused children. The photos had been taken by the police department at the time the children were brought to be placed with social services. Those photos were brutally graphic. Probably none of the listeners had ever seen anything like it. Probably none of the listeners would have believed that any human being could inflict that much injury on a helpless child. Were the photos a distraction? Of course they were. But the impact and support for the message far outweighed the distraction.

The decision is yours. You must decide what visuals, if any, will help your listeners understand, accept, or do what you promote.

23. Restate Ideas in a Variety of Ways

Restatement is the art of being redundant without being repetitious. To restate is not to merely repeat the same thing in the same way; to restate is to find different ways of communicating a message. Using a variety of types of support—an example, a quotation, a comparison with a statistic—to develop an idea affords a likelihood that more of our listeners will understand or embrace our ideas.

Restatement gives us a chance to catch a listener's attention with our second support if he "took a mental break" when we mentioned the first support. Restatement recognizes the different experiences and needs of various listeners. What is relevant for one may have little meaning for another. According to Waldo W. Braden, "We communicate—not by what we say, but by what listeners hear." By saying things in a variety of ways, it is likely that a wider part of our audience will hear our message in a way that is meaningful to them.

24. *Organize Ideas for Easy Understanding*

Effective speakers recognize the importance of organization. You've got an important goal—a message you want your listeners to understand, believe, or act on. You have good main points and you've selected great supports to develop your ideas. Now organize your message clearly and it's far more likely that your listeners will understand your message, accept your message, remember your message, and be interested in your message. Are you apt to be interested in something you don't understand? How hard will you work to make sense out of a speech that is hard to follow? If you don't see the speaker's point, you will probably soon take a mental exit. Your listeners are no different. Some speeches are nothing more than a lot of thoughts on a given topic strung together. These "stream of consciousness" presentations are an affront to the audience.

The arrangement you select will depend on your goal, your topic, and your audience. Sound familiar? It's back to your audience analysis to determine what your listeners need in order to follow your ideas. Also, some arrangements will work better for certain topics than for others. Some methods of organization are great for speeches to inform, but weak for a persuasive goal. The following secrets will divulge four of the most useful formats for organizing informational speeches—one of these may be used for a speech to inform or persuade—and four additional methods for constructing persuasive speeches.

25. *Put Your Ideas in Sequential Order*

Some speeches lend themselves to a chronological or sequential ordering. If you are talking about how to do something—especially the steps to take—a sequential ordering is a natural.

If your focus is on an historical event or a process, choose a chronological ordering of ideas. These would be ideal formats for topics like:

- an analysis of the events leading up to the War of 1812

- tracing the invention of the airplane

- tracing the progress of a bill through Congress

- following the process of assembling the components of a computer

- explaining how our currency is engraved and printed

- showing how to reassemble a carburetor

You may even decide to present your ideas in a reverse chronological order, selecting the most recent thing and moving backward in time. If you are introducing a speaker, for example, you may wish to initially mention her present position and then move backward as you highlight her past accomplishments. A sequential order is especially useful for speeches to inform.

26. Put Your Ideas in Spatial Order

If your topic deals with the physical arrangement of things or shows the relationship of parts to the whole, ordering your message according to space considerations may be a perfect fit. Spatial order might showcase your message if you were trying to show:

- the layout of exhibits in the Louvre Museum in Paris

- the flow of passengers from the Metro, to ticketing, to the departure gate at the new airport

- the best route from San Francisco to Albuquerque

- the arrangement of loads in airplane cargo holds

The spatial arrangement is most useful for speeches designed to inform.

27. Organize Your Ideas By Category

This method of arranging ideas is sometimes called "classification" or "topic" order. It is a friend of the speaker with an informative goal because it is a great "catch-all" category. If you cannot organize your speech any other way, this will probably work for you. Some topics just naturally fall into this format.

In talking about the Federal government, you could easily divide your talk by discussing the three branches: the executive, the legislative, and the judicial. But be sure to narrow your focus or you'll have far too much for time limits.

28. Discuss a Problem and Its Solution

Unlike those we've looked at thus far, this method can be used whether your goal is to inform or persuade. You need to first establish the scope of the problem. Go back to your audience analysis to determine whether your listeners are aware of the scope or severity of the problem. Operationally define the problem, if necessary, and stress its importance by describing the severity or impact of the problem.

Any solution you present will involve expenditures—either of people's time or money. To be convinced to accept **any** solution, listeners must be first convinced there is a significant problem that needs solving. Problems are perceived to be significant if a large number of people are impacted or if the impact is very severe on those affected. Don't move too rapidly from a discussion of the problem to your presentation of solutions.

The second step is to present several solutions if your goal is to inform. Discuss each proposed solution in order that your listeners take with them an awareness of the choices and pros and cons of each. If your goal is to persuade, you will probably spend most of your time on the one solution you are promoting and build supports as to why it is the best solution. You may chose to mention the other solutions competing for acceptance in order to explain why those are inferior to the solution you are advocating.

29. Provide Listeners a Statement of Reasons

This method is appropriate when your goal is to persuade and you believe your audience essentially agrees with your point of view or is undecided about the issue. The method is a form of the "category order" in which each main point is a reason justifying your goal statement.

Take, for example, the issue of refinancing home mortgages during a period of low interest rates. Your general goal statement is:

"To convince my listeners to refinance now before interest rates go higher."

This statement serves as the basis for the following four examples of how to organize the main ideas of a speech to persuade. You can use the problem solution or any of the remaining four methods for organizing this speech. Each method constitutes a separate secret of highly effective speakers—#29, 30, 31, and 32. Of course, adequate supporting materials and development of each point would be needed for any of the speeches to be effective.

> **Goal:** I want my listeners to agree that they should now refinance their home mortgages with ABC Mortgage.

> I. If your current fixed 30-year mortgage rate is above 8½ percent, you can save thousands of dollars over the term of your loan given current low interest rates.

> II. You can refinance your present mortgage with little or no cash and immediately lower your monthly payments.

> III. The refinancing process is quick and easy—you can begin the refinancing process tomorrow and begin paying the lower rate with your next mortgage payment.

Notice that each main point is a reason why the listeners should refinance now.

30. *Provide Listeners With Comparative Advantages*

This method outlines reasons why it is most advantageous to do what the speaker proposes. This method works especially well when you know many members of your audience agree with your arguments. The arguments presented usually emphasize why it is better to take action according to the speaker's plan:

Goal: I want my listeners to agree that they should now refinance their home mortgages with ABC Mortgage.

I.   ABC Mortgage offers a fixed 30-year interest rate of 6½ percent—lower than any other company.

II. A special refinancing package this month will eliminate costly points and other standard loan processing fees charged by other companies.

III. ABC Mortgage guarantees a 24-hour response to your loan application—the fastest in the business.

Notice that each reason states what the listener should agree with or do in terms of its advantage over the other options.

31. Use the Criteria-Satisfaction Method

This method attempts to build a consensus amongst members of a somewhat hostile audience. The approach initially tries to get individuals to agree to the speaker's points.

Goal: I want my listeners to agree that they should now refinance their home mortgages with ABC Mortgage.

I.   As homeowners, we all want to know when we sign for our mortgage that we have the best deal possible.

A. We all want to pay the lowest interest rate.
B. We all want to put up as little cash as possible at settlement.

     C. We all want an application process that is
        quick and easy.

The speaker has made statements he believes his listeners will agree with. He believes they all want the lowest rate possible and will say a mental "yes." He believes they will agree they want to pay as little cash as possible on the deal and would like an easy application process. Once he has their "yes" response, he moves on and indicates how his company's mortgage package meets each of the goals the listeners have already agreed they favor.

   II.   ABC Mortgage is offering the best deal in today's
        marketplace.

     A. ABC Mortgage's fixed 30-year 6½ percent
        rate is the lowest available.
     B. With ABC Mortgage you need little or no
        cash at settlement.
     C. ABC Mortgage's application process is quick
        and easy to complete.

This can be a very effective method with audiences in initial disagreement with the speaker's goal. Of course, each of the main points needs to be developed to support the ideas you present.

32. Use the Negative Method

This method is viable for hostile audiences to persuade them to agree with the speaker's arguments. Here you show that the alternatives available to your listeners are less advantageous to them than the proposal you are advocating.

Goal: I want my listeners to agree that they should now refinance their home mortgages with ABC Mortgage.

   I. Keeping your present mortgage at over 8½ percent is a poor financial strategy.

  II. Waiting for interest rates to go lower than our 6½ percent offer is misplaced optimism.

 III. Taking out a variable rate mortgage is equivalent to playing Russian Roulette with your financial future.

 IV. Refinancing with a fixed 30-year mortgage at 6½ percent with ABC Mortgage is the only choice of wise money managers.

Notice how the speaker points out that each of the three other options the audience may consider are just not good choices. Their best alternative is to do what the speaker advocates.

Command Attention—Your Introduction Sets the Tone

THE FIRST WORDS OUT OF EVERY SPEAKER'S mouth should be a well planned attempt to gain listeners' attention. What a lost opportunity if the first sentence is, "Can everyone hear me?" or "Today I'm going to talk about..." These are "ho-hum" rather than "lend me your ears" beginnings. Once your listeners take a mental exit, it is difficult to get them back in the room. The rest of the speech, no matter how strong, will be an uphill struggle to regain their attention. However, if you start strong and capture attention at the beginning, you have an excellent chance of keeping listeners with you if your message is well adapted to your audience.

In addition to grabbing attention, your introduction must relate to your speech topic so you can smoothly transition to your message. The introduction attempts to gain attention, but then focuses that attention on the theme of the speech. Your first goal is to reach out and capture your listeners' attention. So if, "Today I'm going to talk about. . ." is dull, what are better ways to begin?

33. *Refer to the Subject or Occasion*

If there is anything special about the occasion—it marks the 40th anniversary of the Peace Corps or celebrates the successful completion of the fund raising drive for the National Symphony —you may choose to begin your speech by alluding to the occasion itself. It is an opportunity to build cohesion within the group and your rapport with them, especially if you are an outsider, as you congratulate them on their fine work or mark the milestone.

►*Caution!*

If you present a weak introduction that causes your audience to make a "mental exit," it's nearly impossible to get them back into the room.

34. *Begin With a Powerful Quotation*

A quotation used in the body of the speech is selected for its support. A quotation used to begin should be selected for its impact. The quotation or the source should be sufficient to pique listeners' interest. Or, the fact that the audience does not know **initially** that it is a quote may be an attention grabber in itself. Take, for example, the 18-year old college student who approached the lectern and began saying:

> "'I have today signed an Executive Order providing for the Establishment of a Peace Corps on a temporary pilot basis. I am also sending to Congress a message proposing

authorization of a permanent Peace Corps. This Corps will be a pool of trained American men and women sent overseas by the U.S. Government or through private institutions and organizations to help foreign countries meet their urgent needs for skilled manpower.'(brief pause)These were the words of President John F. Kennedy on March 1, 1961, when he signed into law the Peace Corps."

That this was a quote was not initially revealed to the listeners. Imagine the audience looking at this 18-year old and wondering, what does he mean, he has signed an executive order? What does he mean when he says he recommends to Congress? Who does he think he is? It got listeners' attention as it was intended to do, and provided the segue to an informative talk about the Peace Corps.

35. Ask a Rhetorical Question

If a rhetorical question is posed and listeners hear it, they almost certainly will answer it—to themselves. They have no choice. As listeners respond—to themselves—they become less passive listeners. As they become more active participants in the communication, their attention is focused on your message.

A rhetorical question is posed for thought and internal response. The speaker neither expects hands to be raised nor answers to be shouted out. The speaker may pose one or a series of questions. Look at the following introduction which uses a series of questions to gain attention:

"Did you know, when you got up this morning and stood naked ready to step into the shower, you were already wearing 7 to 10 of your very best colors? When you dressed, did you attire yourself to complement and enhance those body colors or to overpower them? Do you look best in a pure white blouse or shirt, or is a slightly creamy white more flattering? Can you wear your white with a navy suit and look authoritative and powerful, or does that much contrast overpower you? Should you wear jewelry of bright, highly polished metals, or does a matte finish enhance your natural coloring more? These are questions you may have never even considered, yet alone answered. By the time you leave here today, you will be able to answer these and many other questions that relate to your very best look for both business and social occasions."

The speaker then delivered a speech demonstrating how each person could best select and combine their colors to enhance their own natural coloring using the Color 1 system.

Note that these are rhetorical questions posed to the audience with the intention that the listeners will respond internally. If ever you consider asking questions to which you want the audience members to make an actual response—especially early in your speech—think again. Consider two inherent problems. First, you lose control of the direction and focus. A question posed by an audience member may take off on a tangent you neither want nor are prepared to follow. Second, even if you are able to refocus in the direction you wish to take your listeners, it will have taken precious time.

36. *Make a Startling Statement*

You may vie for your listeners' attention by beginning your speech with a statement that will startle them. If they hear you, they cannot help but listen to hear what will come next. The following opening got listeners' attention for a speaker whose goal was to convince the audience that the "good old days" weren't really as good as many of us believe:

> "A loaf of bread costs just 14¢, the price of a gallon of milk is 43¢—and that is delivered to your door! An average new car costs $802 and the median asking price for a house in Washington, D.C., is $12,309. The year is 1948. Sound good? Wish we could return to the 'good ole days'? Go back to those low prices? But wait a minute. Want to know what your salary would be? The average annual salary for a college teacher was $4,123. A non-salaried lawyer might earn $5,700. If you were a dentist, you might make $5,900. And if you were a woman, you could probably forget about even coming close to those figures!"

Or consider the following first line to open a speech to employees or to stockholders in which the speaker's purpose is to tout the growth and accomplishments of the firm:

> "Today we just shipped the 6 millionth book out our door."

A speaker began a speech on conservation by juxtaposing the following two short sentences:

> "One tree can make a million matches. But one match can destroy a million trees."

The following opening line was used by a speaker whose goal was to actuate listeners to use their seat belts and make sure everyone in the car had their seat belts fastened before the car left the driveway:

> "I don't wish to unduly alarm you, but I feel it is only
> fair for me to warn you that by this time next year, one
> of you people sitting in the audience tonight will be
> dead."

The speaker then went on to cite the number of deaths related
to traffic accidents each year. He explained that, with the
number of people present, though he could not predict that one
of the actual audience members would die, within the year
statistically one person from a group of that size would be killed
in an auto accident.

A startling statement is meant to grab the listeners' attention. If the listeners hear the statement, they will be compelled
to perk up their ears to see what this means for them. Obviously, the speaker must be able to make the connection
between the startling statement and the thrust of the speech.

37. Keep Listeners in Suspense

Entice your listeners by **briefly** keeping them in suspense. You
are providing a hook for your listeners as they try to guess what
you are leading up to. You must keep the use of suspense short.
If you keep listeners in suspense too long, you will lose—not
heighten—their interest. First, let's look at an example that
most listeners were probably able to guess before the speaker
told them:

> "It has 88 keys, but no locks; 230 strings, but you
> couldn't fly a kite with it. Twenty million people play it,
> but it isn't a game. It's the piano—America's most
> popular musical instrument. The National Piano Foun-
> dation has designated September as National Piano
> Month. This seems an appropriate time for me to .... "

Not difficult—most listeners anticipated what was being referred to, but it was intriguing and caught their attention. The next example is short and combines the use of suspense with a question:

> "What do the telephone, airline, and electric utility industries have in common? After a decade of dramatic change, all three industries have been deregulated. What does this mean for us as consumers and as investors?"

38. Engage Listeners With a Vivid Illustration

Everyone enjoys a good story well told. You can make it personal. Your audience will enjoy hearing about something that happened to you. Or you can tell a story about someone else. You will recall that Ronald Reagan, when he was president, often sprinkled his talks with stories about everyday people whose situation helped him make a point or gain attention. Several presidents since have also made use of this technique to connect with their listeners. If you have a story to tell that is especially powerful and relates to the focus of your speech, use it. A recent seminar participant related the following personal incident:

> "I'm going to tell you a story. It's the story of a rescue. It was the winter of 1979, and it was a particularly cold night. The weather forecasters on television kept re-minding listeners to bring their pets in and that no one should go out unless it was absolutely necessary, because with the wind chill factor the temperature was something like -70°.
>
> It was about 7pm on a Friday night and my first

husband, Riley, and I were in the living room standing by the front door when all of a sudden I said, 'Let's go to Wendy's.' (Wendy's—the fast food place.) As soon as I said, 'Let's go to Wendy's' I immediately thought to myself that I didn't really want to go to Wendy's and I had no idea why I would say such a thing on a night like this. Riley's eyes got real big and he looked at me like I had said, 'Let's fly to the moon.' But he was always ready for adventure.

So we put our daughter, Michelle, in her car seat in the back of my little Mustang and set out. It was very cold. Riley commented that he hoped the Mustang didn't conk out because, if it did, he would never be able to get it started again in that cold weather. I kept wondering what in the world we were doing going to Wendy's on a cold night like that.

It was very dark and the windows of the Mustang were fogged over from the cold. I kept staring out my window as best I could when suddenly I saw a car that was pulled over to the side of the road. I noticed that there was someone in the car. I said to Riley, 'There's someone in that car.' We drove for a couple of seconds and I said, 'They're going to freeze to death.' Riley said, 'Someone will stop and pick them up.' I said, 'What if no one stops . . . they will freeze.' This conversation went on a minute or two and then we decided to go back and make sure the person in the car had gotten rescued.

We pulled off at the next exit, circled around and started back. Because we had to get back on and off the interstate it took us about 20 minutes to get back to the stranded car. Riley pulled the Mustang just in front of that car, left the motor running because it was so cold, and got out. Riley got about halfway to the other car when a woman jumped out of the car, ran up to Riley and grabbed him around the waist—just as a drowning person would grab someone who had jumped into the water to save them. Riley had to pry her loose; then he walked over to her car, lifted the hood, and worked on the car for a few minutes. The car didn't have enough anti-freeze and the carburetor had ice crystals in it. Riley got the car started and told the woman to follow us to the nearest gas station. Once there Riley added anti-freeze and put gas in her car. Then we went on to Wendys'.

There was a very young baby in that car with the woman. The baby had on only a lightweight stretch outfit and no blanket. I have decided that the sole reason we went to Wendy's was to rescue that woman and her baby. Neither Riley nor I really wanted to go to Wendy's that night and we didn't enjoy eating there because we were so worried about the Mustang freezing. I think God picked us to rescue that woman because not many other people would have been foolish enough to go out on a night like that, because He knew we would see the woman's car and He knew Riley would have no trouble getting her car started."

This is longer than many introductions, but then stories take time to tell. If there is sufficient time to make a transition to the theme of the speech and build the supports for the main ideas, an introduction of this length is acceptable. The important things are that it capture the listeners' attention and that the speaker be able to build on that for the remainder of the speech.

39. Hit Listeners With a Humorous Anecdote

The use of a joke to begin a speech is one of the most over-worked and most misused ways to begin. It is probably over-worked because many speakers don't know any other way. Now that you know several other methods to introduce your speech, if you chose to begin with a joke it should be a strong opener—not a default.

A joke is misused when it in no way relates to the message of the speech. It doesn't set the stage for the listeners or prepare them for your information or persuasion if it is irrelevant to the focus of your speech. A joke is also misused if it is offensive to any of your listeners. Carefully consider the audience you expect in attendance, and avoid any material that might offend any of them. You need to build bridges in your introduction: a bridge to your message as well as a bridge of good feeling and rapport between your listeners and you, the speaker. Why would you break that bond by alienating any member of your audience?

 **► Caution!**

Be careful in using a joke to begin your speech. This overworked and often misused method may offend some listeners. Carefully consider your audience before engaging in humor.

Consider the following opening to a speech by John Howard about curing an unrecognized malady afflicting private enter-prise.

"A story is told of a knight who returned to his castle at twilight. He was a mess. His armor was dented, his helmet was askew, his face was bloody, his horse was limping, the rider was listing to one side in the saddle. The Lord of the castle saw him coming and went out to meet him, asking, 'What hath befallen you, Sir Knight?' Straightening himself up as best he could, he replied, 'Oh, Sire, I have been laboring in your service, robbing and pillaging your enemies to the west.' 'You've been WHAT? cried the startled nobleman, 'but I haven't any enemies to the west!' 'Oh!' said the knight. And then after a pause, 'Well, I think you do now.'"

The point of the story was, of course, that enthusiasm was not enough—one has to have a sense of direction. The thrust of the speech was that business needed to know who its enemies were and focus its defenses on the right targets.

Even though humor is often misused, it can be effective if used appropriately. Ask yourself these questions:

- Is the humor related to the focus of the speech? Or can I make the explicit connection?

- Will the material be humorous to this audience?

- Is my delivery style such that I can make it humorous to this audience?

- Am I sure the humor will not offend **anyone** in my audience?

- Is this the best attention getter for this speech and this audience?

If you can answer yes to each of the five questions, the use of humor ought to be a viable choice. Make humor work to gain your listeners' attention and then transition to the focus of your speech.

40. Orient Your Listeners

The first aspect of formulating an introduction to command attention is to pique your listeners' interest; the second is to let your listeners know, early in the speech, your direction and focus. The transition between the attention step and the main ideas you present should be tightly focused and to the point. The following was the transition John Howard used following the humorous anecdote about the misdirected knight:

> "There is a moral to this story. Enthusiasm is not enough. You have to have a sense of direction. Private enterprise, like the bedraggled knight, is not at its best these days. This morning I want to pose to you the possibility that the troubles which beset the business community may arise because it does not have a very clear idea of who its opponents are and, as a result, is focusing much of its defensive energies upon the wrong targets. The sense of direction is amiss."

The speaker is now poised to launch his main ideas and develop their supports.

41. Build Rapport

Not every speech needs special efforts to build rapport with listeners. But you should take a moment to consider whether this is a need for **this** speech, to **this** audience, by **this** speaker—you. Whether you spend any time at all, or what proportion of your speech you devote to establishing common ground between you and your listeners will depend upon your audience analysis. Are your listeners likely to be "hostile" toward either you or your goal? If yes, you **must** devote effort to build rapport.

If you were in the audience with a speaker whom you disliked personally, disliked the organization he represented, or disliked his viewpoint, you would be filled with negative thoughts. You might be convinced you would not agree with anything this "misinformed" individual might say. If he simply launches pell-mell into his speech, you will probably be right! Chances are you will dig your heels in and disagree with everything.

But how this scenario changes if the speaker establishes common ground with his listeners. This can often be done by moving back from specifics and looking at the general. Speaker and listeners almost always have basic things in common and can reach agreement at that level.

Success Tip

If facing a hostile audience, begin your speech by establishing common ground—present something you all agree upon.

For example, as I was writing the first edition of this book, the school system in Washington, D.C. was late for the second year in a row in getting the school year underway. Most surrounding area schools began classes on September 2nd, but the District was scheduled to begin classes on September 22nd—three weeks late. There was some question whether there might be even further delays. The reason? Repairs needed to be made to the buildings—most notably to the roofs. No one was happy with the situation and everyone had someone to blame for the state of affairs. The disagreement was rampant. What could everyone agree on in this situation? They all wanted the best possible education and in the safest surroundings for their children. The disagreement was not on the end, but on the means for getting there.

A speaker who would move immediately to a discussion of

her solution to the problem would be foolish, because surely it will antagonize a significant number of listeners and would be almost doomed to failure from the start. However, if the speaker were to begin by establishing common ground, talking first about the things she and her listeners could agree on, she would have a chance of being effective.

Speaking in a televised ad a few years ago for a Virginia election campaign, Chuck Robb in support of Doug Wilder said he and Mr. Wilder agreed "on the important things like educating our children and building a better life for Virginia families." How many people in the television audience do you suppose were against either of these goals?

Find the basic things you and your listeners will agree on. Start with those. You want your listeners to say internally, "Gee, this person isn't as bad as I thought she was. I didn't think we would agree on anything. But our views aren't so different after all." At this point the audience is ready to really listen and you have a chance to make your case. If your main ideas and supports are also well developed for this audience, you may find you are effective in a situation where most speakers would be beaten before they had begun!

Another method that can be effective is to ask a series of rhetorical questions to which you are certain your listeners will respond with an internal "yes."

"Do you want your child to have the best possible education?"

"Do you want your child to do well in school?"

"Do you want your child to have available the tools, right in your home, to help him excel?

What parent wouldn't answer "yes" to each of these questions? A decade or more ago, when encyclopedia salespeople set up appointments to go into homes to make their sales pitch, these were the kinds of questions they would ask. If the salesperson could get the prospective buyer to answer "yes" several times, they knew they had a greater likelihood of a "yes" response when it came time to close the sale. Why? In part because a pattern of "yes" responses was being established. The habit was to respond in the affirmative. But the salesperson was also building rapport by establishing common ground.

Effective speakers attempt to establish common ground with their listeners when speaking to potentially hostile audiences. They help their listeners identify with them and realize they have similar goals. By emphasizing their areas of agreement, speakers stand a better chance that their audience will listen with an open mind and may be persuaded to accept the speaker's point of view.

42. Provide Explicit Motivation

What makes you pay attention to a speaker? His enthusiasm for his message? The language he uses? The variety of his inflection? His sense of humor? His sensitivity to the audience? All of these things probably are factors influencing your level of attention. But the bottom-line motivation is the answer to the question, "What's in it for me?"

When you were a student you listened to some pretty dreadful lectures, didn't you? You actually paid money for the privilege of going to class and listening to the boring monologues delivered in monotones. Why? You wanted the credit hours and you wanted a decent grade on your transcript. You had motivation—even though it wasn't necessarily the knowledge that was the motivator.

If it isn't already obvious to your audience what the payoff will be for them, tell them up front why this is important to them:

- Will they make the best decision as to which health plan to opt for at their place of employment?

- Will they be able to negotiate a higher salary at their next performance and salary review?

- Will they make better investments that will increase their money in the stock market?

- Will they learn how to save the life of a loved one in the event they stop breathing?

- Will they know better how to negotiate the best deal on a used car?

- Will they lose weight and maintain a healthier life-style?

Whatever the advantage to your listeners, stress the payoff early in your speech—especially if there is any doubt whether they are aware of the importance of the message you are presenting and the ramifications to their lives.

43. Establish Credibility

If your speech is addressed to people who know you well, your credibility—whether high or low—is already established with your audience. However, if you speak to audiences that have little information about you, the speaker, you want to establish your credibility. Audiences will pay greater attention to a speaker whom they regard as having expertise and being trustworthy —two of the major components of credibility.

How can you build your credibility in the eyes of your audience?

- If someone is to introduce you, their introduction may be sufficient to provide your listeners with information about your qualifications and accomplishments so that they will view you as a highly credible source and give to you their full attention. See Secret #54 on how to ensure that the person who introduces you includes the qualifications you want emphasized.

- If there is to be no one who makes an introduction, it is especially important for you to subtly weave into your early remarks comments that demonstrate what qualifies you to speak on the topic. Make these comments early in your speech —but after the attention-getting step of your introduction—so the attention your listeners give you will be heightened. People pay better attention to speakers to whom they attribute high credibility. For example, if you look younger than you are and are constantly seen as a neophyte in your company/industry when in fact you have many years of experience, the following comment could allay the mistaken impression:

    "In the fifteen years I have been with MYCO, it has been my experience that . . ."

That single statement could make the difference between listeners daydreaming through your presentation or realizing early in your speech that you must have a lot more experience than they thought you had, as they had based their impressions on your youthful appearance. You can use the same approach if you have a special credential:

> "Last March when I testified before the Senate committee on . . ."

Comments such as these can add to your stature in the view of your listeners, making them more likely to pay attention to what you say as well as more likely to be open to new ideas or ideas that differ from their point of view. Weaving these credibility enhancers subtly into remarks you make early in your speech builds credibility without appearing pretentious.

Secrets #33 through #39 suggested several ways you might choose from to formulate introductions to command listeners' attention. These methods are great starting points, but don't limit yourself to these options. Consider your goal, your audience, your message, your own strengths as a speaker, and you may devise a more perfect introduction for your unique goal than any of the suggestions here. Let me share with you what one student did that was perfect for his particular speech:

> The assignment had been to give a speech to demonstrate. Dan volunteered as the final speaker of the day. As he strode to the front of the room with a baseball in one hand and a glove in the other hand, no doubt the entire class had expectations of a speech on some aspect of how to play baseball. When Dan got to the front of the classroom, he put the baseball glove down, and with a flourish pitched the baseball through the window—

which was closed. At this point he had the attention of everyone in the room!

Dan went on to explain that he had spent the prior summer working in a plate glass company. Prior to that experience he'd had no idea how often people needed to have a pane of glass replaced—either because someone had inadvertently tossed or batted a ball through a window, or the occupants had locked themselves out and had broken a pane to let themselves into the house. Dan indicated that it frequently took a day or more before someone from the glass company could get out to replace a broken pane of glass. "But," he continued, "it is easy to replace it yourself and normally if you'll give the dimensions of the glass to the glass company they can cut it for you and you can replace it the very same day." He added that in addition to the time saved, the homeowner could save money as well. He then proceeded to show the class how to remove the shards and replace the broken pane of glass.

Dan had adroitly gotten the attention of his audience; he let his listeners know the focus of his speech; he established his credibility; and he gave his listeners motivation for their attention. He did not attempt to build rapport, because his audience analysis suggested this was not necessary. Dan's was a perfect introduction for **this** speech. It would fit few others.

Use the suggested attention getters in secrets #34 through #40 as possibilities for your speeches, but don't let them limit you. There are other potential openers that you may devise which can be unique and special for achieving your goal. Think of your purpose and you may create a very special opening that will literally command the attention of every listener in the room.

Close With Power

MANY SPEAKERS DON'T KNOW HOW TO CON-clude a talk. They've worked on the message they want to present, and perhaps they have given thought to an introduction, but they give little or no thought to how they will finish. I have heard many speakers get to the end of their message and conclude with, "That's all." I don't know about the rest of the audience, but I tend to visualize the cartoon character at the end of the Looney Tunes Cartoons waving at the audience and saying in a high pitched voice, "That's all, folks." This is **not** a power closing.

The other frequent end to a speech is for the speaker to ask, "Are there any questions?" There are plenty of occasions when it may be appropriate, desirable, and even expected that there will be an opportunity for the audience to pose questions. However, this should not be confused as a substitute for a conclusion. Rather, the opportunity for questions to be asked should be an additional step. A question-and-answer session is

not a power closing. In fact, as soon as you open the floor to questions from the audience you relinquish control over the focus. You may find that a listener's question takes you and the rest of the audience off on a tangent. If you prepare by following Secret #52, you will be able to both regain the focus you have chosen for your speech **and close with power**!

Communication studies indicate listeners remember best the beginning and end of a speech. In fact, as soon as a speaker says, "In conclusion . . . ," listeners will perk up their ears. So take advantage of the heightened attention you will have as you conclude your presentation. You want to both focus the audience attention on the main thrust or goal of your speech and leave them with a memorable statement. Once you conclude your speech, walk back to your seat with the same demeanor of confidence with which you approached the podium to begin.

 **Caution!**

Avoid "That's all" and "Are there any questions?" closings. These are weak closings that diminish the power of your presentation.

44. *Summarize Your Main Points*

This is your opportunity to hit your listeners for the final time with the main thrust of your talk or a succinct summary of the main points. Take advantage of it! Focus listeners' heightened attention where you want it to be. Though we'll look at delivery secrets a bit later, it is worth noting that if your goal is persuasive, this is a point to be especially dynamic in your delivery— your conviction is itself a powerful persuader. Your summary of main points is the first power tool of your speech closing.

The summary of your main points focuses listener attention, but in most cases it may not be memorable in a powerful way. So, after summarizing the main points and focusing the audience's attention where you want it to be, utilize the second power tool of your conclusion. You want to leave them with what I call a "statement of impact." This memorable or impact statement has a similar goal to the attention step in the introduction. But rather than gain attention as did the introduction, used in the conclusion this power tool will **retain** audience attention. A strong "statement of impact" will make the speech memorable and better recalled. Any of the methods suggested for getting attention in the introduction, with the exception of suspense, may be used to conclude. Your task is to select the closing you believe will be the most memorable to your audience as well as supportive of your goal.

45. Refer To The Subject or Occasion

Just as a speaker may choose to begin a speech by referring to the occasion, it is possible to close by making reference to the reason the group is gathered. The speaker might also allude to carrying on the work that the organization has been engaged in or looking forward to the next anniversary the group will celebrate and suggesting goals to be met prior to that occasion.

46. End With a Powerful Quotation

The quotation most often is a different quotation or even a different method than the one used in the introduction to the speech. But if you have a really strong quotation, it may be powerful enough to use at both the beginning and the end of your speech. It can tie the speech together and provide unity.

47. Ask a Rhetorical Question

Again, you are asking a question to which you want your listeners to respond internally. You are not asking them to shout out a response or raise their hands to be called upon. By now their internal responses should meet your expectations. Their internal answers should be—whether positive or negative —the ones you expect.

48. Make a Startling Statement

You may choose to close with a startling statement whether or not you used this method for your opening. With a strong startling statement it is even possible to begin and end with the same startling statement. If you use the same statement to both begin and end your speech, make sure you make the decision because you believe the statement to be a really strong and appropriate one for your speech goal. Do not make the decision because it is simply easier for you than formulating a different opening and closing.

49. Leave Listeners With a Vivid Illustration

A strong story vividly told can leave a lasting impression and make your speech and its main thrust memorable.

50. Leave Listeners With a Humorous Anecdote

As was the case with the introduction, be cautious with the use of humor. The humorous story should relate to the focus of your speech; be humorous and told with a delivery style that lends to the humorous nature of the anecdote; and the humor should not be offensive to anyone.

51. *Issue a Challenge or Appeal*

If you have attempted to move your listeners to do something, you may challenge them to meet a goal or appeal to them to take action. Warren W. Wiggins, former deputy director and a philosophical guiding force of the Peace Corps, ended a speech on the celebration of the 25th anniversary of the Peace Corps with a challenge to his audience:

> "You and I and the Al Ulmer's of this decade are a part of the larger establishment. We cannot look to the Pied Pipers and their Gramm-Rudman-Hollings answers. We must look to ourselves. There is no doubt that those of us assembled here could beat a different drum, and with the leverage that **is** ours, **should we grasp it**, like Archimedes, we could move the world."

52. *Keep a Second Closing in Reserve*

You have planned a summary of your main points and you have a "statement of impact" to close your presentation. But you are not finished yet. Prepare a second "statement of impact" and keep it in reserve. You will be prepared to conclude with your first summary followed with your "statement of impact." Then if there is a to be a question-and-answer session, it will be conducted by either you, the speaker, or the moderator—if there is one.

At the end of the questions, you are **not** going to just thank the audience and sit down. To do that would not be memorable; it would not be powerful; and very likely it would not leave your listeners with the focus you had intended. You want to take back the floor, the focus, and the force. You do this by closing with the second conclusion you are holding in reserve. Present this second conclusion and you not only have a memorable close, you add polish and professionalism as well.

Prepare Like a Pro

A "PRO" IS PREPARED, PROFESSIONAL, AND POLished. The twelve secrets that follow will help you be thoroughly prepared, from becoming familiar with and modifying the speaking environment to your advantage; preparing the person who will introduce you to the audience with your relevant accomplishments; tips for preparing your notes or manuscript so you deliver your speech easily; to anticipating questions that are likely to come from your audience. These activities, paired with the secrets to help you control fear and sharpen delivery, can make the difference between just "getting through" a speech and making an effective and polished presentation.

53. *Check the Speaking Environment Prior To Your Presentation*

Secret #5 suggested you consider elements pertaining to the situation in which you would deliver your speech. That analysis was to help you plan for your speech as you put it together. At this point in your preparations, you need to conduct a thorough check of the environment where you will present your speech and seek to modify those elements of the situation you wish to have changed and adapt to those that are unchangeable. Check the room yourself, if you can. If the presentation is to be in another city, talk with someone who has actually been in the room. Have specific questions you ask:

■ Is there a stage area?

■ If there is a stage or raised platform, how high is it?

■ Is there special lighting that will be focused on the speaking area?

■ Is there a lectern or a podium? Is it open so I can move around it freely?

■ Is there a microphone? Fixed or lavaliere? Do I really need a mike in this room?

■ What audio-visual equipment is available? Any special placement required?

■ How many people will the room hold?

■ How is the seating arranged?

■ Can the chairs be moved, or are they bolted to the floor?

■ What is the temperature like in the room? Can I control it? How?

- What is the noise level (from other rooms or outside) in the room?

These are some of the situational constraints you may wish to check personally or ask about. Formulate your own list. Add any special concerns you have about your speaking environment.

54. Change Environmental Elements To Fit Your Style & Goal

As soon as possible, check the environment where you will present your speech. If you check on the situational constraints early enough, you may be able to change elements of the situation to better fit your presentation style or your speaking goal.

If the room size, arrangement for audience seating, noise level, or other conditions that cannot be altered are not conducive to your style or goals, it may be possible to change the room assignment if you begin early. If, however, you wait until a day or two prior to your presentation to find the problem, you are likely to be stuck with it. If you are comfortable moving out from behind the lectern occasionally as you speak and enjoy the closer interaction with the audience this less formal style affords, you may try to change the presentation venue if your designated space puts you behind a fairly enclosed podium. If you want your listeners to interact with one another and hence need a room with movable seating so the audience can break out into small groups, it may be imperative to change rooms if you are assigned one with immovable seating. Determine the elements of the situation early and you have a good chance of making a change you deem necessary. Wait until the last minute and you are probably stuck with what you've got.

Always request any items such as a lectern, audio-visual equipment, an extension cord, or other materials you need. Follow up a few days before the presentation to make certain the requested items will be available. If you ship things for your presentation to another location, call ahead and to be sure of the name of the person you will ship to; then call to verify the shipment has been received. Especially if the shipment goes to a hotel, get the name of the person on staff who will be expecting it. That person should see that the shipment is stored where it can be retrieved on your arrival.

55. *Prepare Your "Introducer" With An Introduction*

If you are fortunate to have someone make a formal introduction of you to your audience, make the most of this opportunity. You want your listeners to think as highly of you, your qualifications, and accomplishments as possible. The initial attention they give to you will be directly related to how they feel about you—your expertise as well as whether they trust you. Since you can't go around saying how great you are, let the person who introduces you do it for you.

I recently attended a meeting—the first one of the fall season—and watched the speaker be introduced in such a way that she got no mileage out of the introduction at all. Rather than tout the speaker's accomplishments and indicate why she was qualified to give the speech she was about to deliver, the introducer talked about how she had issued the invitation to the speaker the previous spring. Then near the end of the summer she tried and tried to contact the speaker and could not reach her. Until a few days before the meeting she was unsure whether the speaker would show up at all!

I am sure the uncertainty as to whether the speaker would be back in town at the end of her summer break in time to speak at the meeting was unsettling to the person who was responsible for the program. But relating this chain of events to the audience did nothing to enhance the speaker's qualifications or to make us want to hear the speaker!

If someone is to introduce you, list your qualifications and accomplishments—those that are appropriate to the topic and thrust of your speech, as well as being positive credentials to the particular audience you will address. I would list them as bulleted items rather than try to write out the introduction. This makes it more likely that the person making the introduction will use the items you wish, yet use her own words so that it sounds more naturally like the person making the introduction. It may also save you the embarrassment of having the introducer conclude by saying that she read the introduction exactly as you wrote it!

You may even comment to the person who is to introduce you that you will include only those things you believe will be of interest to the audience as they relate to the speech you will present. Then make two copies. Fax, mail, or give one copy to the person who will make the introduction. Take the second copy with you when you give your speech. The second copy is a back-up. If the person introducing you forgets his copy, you have a second to give him.

The second copy takes no additional time to make, but is a lifesaver when the chairperson has left his at home, the dog ate it, or the CIA confiscated it! You can remain focused on keeping mentally prepared for the speech you are to deliver rather than trying to hastily reconstruct your accomplishments, and the introduction of you and your credentials will not suffer.

56. Select a Title That's a Hit

You do not need a title for every speech you present. If you are making a short presentation at a meeting of your department at work, you probably do not need a speech title. In fact, in such a situation a title might seem overly pompous. Normally you should formulate a title for your speech if there is to be something in print: a printed program, an announcement in the newspaper, or a sign advertising the presentation. You may title your speech if someone is going to introduce you to the audience so the title may be used in the introduction. However, you, the speaker, should not begin by announcing your speech title. Start with the introduction you have prepared.

When selecting a title for your speech, give it careful thought. The title is your advertisement to draw the audience. The title should attempt to gain attention and generate interest in order to entice people to attend your speech. At the same time, the title should honestly portray what the audience can expect to hear. Remember, you have to face the crowd.

 **Caution!**

Be careful in selecting a title for your speech. Don't create unrealistic expectations with a "hyped" title and then disappoint or even anger your audience by not delivering the sizzle. Remember, not all speeches require a title.

If you generate unrealistic expectations you will be left to answer to a disappointed or perhaps an angry audience. The tabloid press are masters of devising titles that generate interest. But when the article fails to live up to the "hype" advertised on the cover, there is no one present on whom the buyer can vent his frustration. Unlike the tabloids at the supermarket check-out, you will be present at the close of your speech. In selecting a title for your speech, you must balance the two goals of generating interest and promising only what you can deliver.

57. Use the 3-Minute Prep For Unexpected Speeches

There are four delivery methods. Three of them require extensive preparation and are the subject of the 58th secret. However, one method, impromptu, is literally without preparation. So this delivery method is not one you would chose. It is thrust upon you in a situation for which you had no advance warning and hence no opportunity to prepare.

Situations like this do occur and may happen to you. You arrive a few minutes before the meeting is to begin and your boss tells you that John, who was supposed to deliver a talk about employees' options in the new pension plan, is sick today. Your boss asks you to make the presentation to the assembled group. This is not a request; it is a command. You don't really have the option of declining because you are not prepared. So what do you do? Do you get nervous as evidenced by the "butterflies" you suddenly feel in your stomach? Does a little voice in your head keep hammering negative thoughts?– "I can't do this. I am going to make a fool of myself. I am going to get up there and nothing but babble is going to come out." Do this and you let your "internal critic" take over. Your critic is that internal voice that tells says you can't do it. You are going to fail. If you allow yourself to indulge in and reinforce such negative thoughts, they may become a self-fulfilling prophecy.

You have a better option: say no to the negativism and let your "internal coach" take over instead. Your coach tells you to make the best of what little time you have to prepare. I make two assumptions for this method to be useful. First, that you have some expertise on the subject. You have probably been working on this project and your boss feels that, next to John, you know the most about the pension plan options. Second, that you can find a minimum of three minutes before you actually begin your presentation. If all else fails, make a short trip to the restroom. You'll probably need that right now anyway!

You will need a piece of paper and a pen—make a habit of always carrying both these items with you. Take the first two minutes to jot down a short phrase noting each of the ideas you think you might cover that are related to the topic and goal. Just brainstorm these ideas quickly. Try to limit your notes to two or three words for each idea and put them in a list form—one under the other. When limiting yourself to two or three words per idea, you'll find that nouns are the most useful triggers. Later when you look down at your notes they will provide a quick mental cue to what you want to talk about. Take that third minute you were allotted for preparation to order your list. You need not rewrite your ideas; just place a number in front of each idea—1, 2, 3—and cross out any ideas you decide to delete.

Use this three-minute prep whenever you have a presentation suddenly thrust upon you. Since it gives the opportunity for some preparation, you will feel more confident and your talk will be more coherent than if you take your other option—which is to do nothing with those three minutes except get nervous! The feedback I get from participants in my seminars who have tried the three-minute prep is that it works wonders! Of course, if you have five or ten minutes for your quick preparation that's even better.

58. Determine Your Delivery Method

The three-minute prep is a great tool for unexpected talks—situations where you have no forewarning of an impending speech. But it is **not** a substitute for the thorough preparation you should engage in for all other occasions—when you do know in advance you will present a speech. For the prepared speech, there are three delivery methods from which to select the one that will best fit both you and your audience:

- extemporaneous

- manuscript

- memorized

Up to this point in your speech preparation, the same amount of effort has been expended—regardless of which delivery method you would use. As you gathered data, selected and organized your main ideas, developed an introduction and conclusion, the steps taken and time spent were the same no matter which delivery method you might later choose. But now you must make a choice of delivery method. Consider the audience—which style will be best suited for them? Consider yourself, the speaker, as well. The amount of time you spend preparing at this step will be affected by the choice you make.

For an **extemporaneous speech** you will make notes consisting of phrases that will jog in your mind each of the points you wish to make and in the order you have planned. As you deliver the speech you will glance at your notes and then talk about each point using the words that come to your mind as you deliver the speech. Many of the phrases you used in your practice sessions will carry over, and you will use them as you present your speech. But much will also vary as you make some points differently each time. This gives the extemporaneous speech the advantage of sounding natural to listeners who are used to hearing this style of speech. It is usually an easy style for the audience to listen to and tends to hold their attention. It also gives the speaker an opportunity to make eye contact with the audience most of the time, note their reactions, and respond to the feedback with clarification or additional support for ideas.

If you chose to deliver a **manuscript speech**, you will need to write out your entire speech word for word. Then you will need to become thoroughly familiar with your manuscript so that you can deliver it smoothly and with as much eye contact with your audience as possible. Because you are tied to the manuscript, it is unlikely that you will make modifications in response to audience feedback. A manuscript speech is a written document delivered orally. The writing style is more formal than the oral style we are used to and hence more difficult for the audience to listen to and understand. Some of the major differences are:

Oral Communication	Written Communication
▪ primarily 1-2 syllable words	▪ greater use of 2, 3, and 4 syllable words
▪ primarily simple sentences	▪ greater use of compound and complex sentences
▪ pause at end of thoughts	▪ pause at punctuation marks
▪ listener can hear only once	▪ reader can go back and re-read

When we read written material, we can go back and re-read sections of material which were unclear. Listeners do not have the opportunity to re-hear your speech. Remember, it is more difficult to listen to the written style of a manuscript than the oral style of an extemporaneous speech.

For a **memorized speech** you will need to write out a manuscript and commit it to memory. A memorized speech retains the disadvantages of a manuscript speech with two additional disadvantages thrown in:

- It is very time consuming to memorize a speech.

- Unless you have a photographic memory, you will live in mortal fear that you will "forget" your speech —and very possibly you will!

So what is the bottom line when deciding whether to select an extemporaneous, manuscript, or memorized delivery to present your speech? Though all three methods involve a significant expenditure of time if you are to "give it your best," the extemporaneous presentation will take the least time to prepare, the manuscript speech will take more of your time than extemporaneous, and the memorized will take the most time of the three to prepare.

So from your perspective as the speaker, the extemporaneous speech delivery, though it still takes time to do it right, will be the least time consuming. You don't have to worry about forgetting your speech, because your notes are there to jog your memory. As long as you don't fall into the trap of thinking you should convey your thoughts in exactly the same words each time you say it, you'll be fine!

From the audience perspective the extemporaneous delivery also comes up a winner. Since it is easier to listen to the oral style, the attention span is better, and with better attention comes better understanding, retention, and a chance for better persuasion. Most individuals who give manuscript speeches do so not because it is the best delivery choice for the situation, but because they are afraid to give up the "crutch" of the written speech. It gives them a sense of security to have the whole speech written out. But the speech that is read is hardly ever as well received by the listeners as an extemporaneous delivery would be. If you, the speaker, are trying to make the choice as to whether to deliver your speech extemporaneously or to read from a manuscript, please remember that **your parents read to you to put you to sleep at night!**

I cannot urge you too strongly to develop your ability to make extemporaneous presentations. In most of the speaking situations you encounter, it will be your best delivery choice. To develop your skill at making extemporaneous presentations is to empower yourself. For otherwise you are likely to continue to give manuscript speeches—not because they are your best choice, but because you feel you have no other option.

Are there any situations where a manuscript speech might be preferred or necessary? If you don't prepare your own speeches, but have a speech writer who prepares them, you will most likely find it difficult to deliver them extemporaneously. What makes the extemp presentation possible is the close contact the speaker has had with the material through the data gathering, selection, and organization stages of preparation. Without this close association throughout the development of their material, most speakers will rely on a manuscript. The best speech writers will write in a style that sounds believable and natural for the intended speaker.

A manuscript, because of its greater use of polysyllabic words and compound and complex sentence structures, will sound more formal. Hence for a formal speech of policy by a head of state, our expectations are met by the tone of the manuscript speech. It is also true that for an important policy speech, where words must be chosen very carefully to avoid misunderstanding, the manuscript allows the speaker to carefully select his words.

Alan Greenspan, Chairman of the Federal Reserve, spoke before the U.S. Congress World Economic Committee on

October 29, 1997. This speech followed currency devaluations by several Asian governments, and stock markets around the world had lost value. Greenspan's audience that day went far beyond the Congressional Economic Committee he was addressing in Washington, D.C. His remarks were listened to carefully by the Asian leaders as well as by investors both in the U.S. and in foreign markets the world over. Although Greenspan knew his subject matter well, he presented his remarks from a manuscript. No doubt his words had been carefully chosen to try to convey a balance between warnings as to what must be done to stabilize those weakened economies, and yet not scare investors into a panic leading to a run on the banks in Asia and markets worldwide.

If a speech is to be broadcast, a manuscript will allow the speaker to better fit the speech into the precise time slot. It is difficult to present an extemporaneous speech and fit it to within a few seconds of a designated time.

Unless you have a photographic memory, I strongly discourage you from memorizing a speech. The likelihood you will forget what you have memorized is great, and you will be likely to be so worried about forgetting it that your delivery will be far less dynamic than it could be if you made a different choice of delivery method.

59. *Prepare Notes (Extemporaneous)*

If you have elected to use an extemporaneous delivery, your next step will be to prepare notes to aid you in delivering your speech. Your notes, if properly formulated, will assure that you will present the points you have selected and in the order you have determined.

Before starting to make notes it is important to determine whether there will be a lectern available and whether you plan to use it. If you will not be using a lectern, put your notes on note cards—preferably at least a 4x6 size. Note cards are preferable to sheets of paper if no lectern will be used. The smaller size is less obtrusive and the heavier weight will be easier to work with if you must hold them as you speak. The 4x6 size will allow you to get more on each card and still leave enough blank space so that your notes will not be too crowded. If you want a bit larger size card you can make them yourself by using cover stock purchased at your local office supply store and cut with a paper cutter.

If you plan to use the lectern, don't put your notes on note cards. Use larger sheets of paper instead. A standard 8½x11 paper size will fit on any lectern I have seen without creeping over the edge of the lectern. In fact two sheets of this size can fit side by side without showing, so as you finish with one sheet you can slide it unobtrusively over to the side. Most lecterns will even handle legal size sheets of paper. The larger sheets of paper will allow you to leave space while placing more information on each page. You will have fewer pages to keep track of and shuffle. The lectern will allow your notes to be unobtrusive and the lighter weight paper stock won't flutter in your hands. Use separate sheets of paper—no paper attached to a notepad or in a notebook. I have seen too many speakers lessen their polished image with yellow notepad paper hanging down the front of the lectern as they turn page after page, or obviously turning pages over in a notebook.

As you construct your notes, use short phrases—preferably no more than two to four words for each of the main ideas and supports you will present. This is a case where "less is more." Many inexperienced speakers start out to make notes and end up with a manuscript! Remember, these notes are to trigger in your mind the ideas you want to convey and keep you focused on the order you have determined is best for your topic, goal, and audience. You will glance down at your notes to check what should come next, but you can look back at your listeners as you deliver the message. If you write out too much you will be afraid to look away from your notes and at your audience. You will be afraid you will have difficulty finding your place in your notes when you next need to check them. Since you have researched, selected, and organized the message, you are familiar with the material. You should only need a short phrase to jog your memory as to the idea you will cover next.

The words you select for the short phrases on your notes should be primarily nouns. Nouns are the single words that will convey the most meaning to jog your thinking as you speak. You need no articles. "The, a, an" and similar words are necessary for complete and smooth sentences when you speak or write, but they only take up precious space as part of the notes you write to trigger in your mind what you wish to say next. Seldom, if ever, will you need conjunctions (and, but), pronouns (he, she, it), or prepositions (over, under, in, out). Occasionally you might use a verb (shows action), an adjective (modifies a noun), or adverb (modifies a verb), but the majority of words should be nouns. For each word you place on your notes, ask yourself whether you really need that word to trigger in your mind what comes next. Don't write out anything more than you absolutely need! Extra verbiage will be your enemy later as you use your notes.

> **Success Tip**

If you slide, rather than flip each page of notes across the lectern as you finish with it, the movement will be less noticeable to the audience.

Whether you are using note cards or sheets of paper, leave lots of space on the paper—between lines, on both sides, at the top and bottom of the page. The more space you leave and the less verbiage you use, the easier it will be to find your place when you need to glance at your notes. Your notes might look something like either of these examples below:

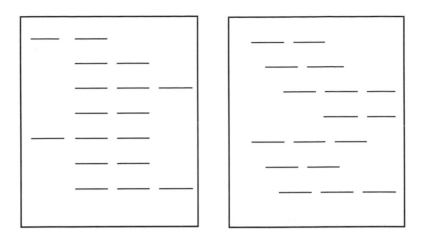

In the first example the notes on the line closest to the left margin would be to trigger the speaker's main idea. The lines indented underneath would be triggers for the supports for that idea. In the second example each line is staggered across the page to help the speaker easily find his place. Chose whichever system works better for you or synthesize the two. I find that unlined note cards or sheets of paper work best. This allows the speaker full control over spacing.

Number your pages. Place a number in one of the corners of each page so that if your pages get out of order—you drop your notes on the way to the lectern—you can quickly put them back in order.

If you have decided to present your speech extemporaneously, make your notes carefully and then **use** them. I don't know why it is, but some speakers seem to believe that the notes are there as a crutch, and that if they can present the speech without referring to their notes it makes them better speakers. Your notes are not a crutch; they are an aid. They are your aid as you present the points you believe this audience will need in order to understand, accept, or do what you have determined is your goal. They are an aid as you present these points in the order that your thoughtful analysis has suggested will be the most effective. Why would you do all the work you have done to this point to carefully craft your message and then take the risk of "blowing it" by not using them?

> **Caution!**
>
> Don't write out anything more than you absolutely need! Extra verbiage will be your enemy later as you use your notes. Use nouns to trigger ideas.

Using notes is not a sign of weakness. It is a sign of a well prepared speaker. Make certain that as you finish talking about the material on each page you move the page you are finished with out of the way. This way, any time you need to glance at your notes the point you are discussing is easy to locate.

60. *Prepare A Manuscript (Manuscript or Memorized)*

If you have chosen to deliver your speech from a manuscript or if you intend to memorize your presentation, you now must actually write your speech word for word. This will be a time-consuming task as you select each word and phrase exactly as you will present it. Put your manuscript on full sheets of paper and use a larger than normal type size. If you have access to desktop-publishing software you can select a type size large enough to be easily read as you stand at the podium, but not so large as to force you to carry a huge sheaf of papers with you. Like the extemporaneous speaker, you want to leave space between lines. Double or triple space your text. Even though you are reading from a manuscript, you need to look at and make eye contact with your audience as frequently as possible. Leaving space between lines in your text will help you find your place as you return to your manuscript.

Although a manuscript speech will sound more formal in language choice and sentence structure than an extemporaneous speech, try to write for the ear. Avoid extremely lengthy sentences. Use a greater number of simple sentences than you ordinarily would if you were writing a piece to be read, and make liberal use of one- and two-syllable words in your speech.

If you write for the ear, you will be rewarded with a more attentive audience. If the listeners are attentive, you are more likely to be effective.

If you choose to deliver your speech from memory, at this point you would take your prepared manuscript and memorize it.

 *Success Tip*

Double- or triple-space the text of a manuscript speech. Maintain good eye contact with your audience even though you are reading from the manuscript.

61. Time Your Speech

At this point in your preparation, talk through an extemporaneous speech or read through a manuscript speech to get an indication of the time it takes to deliver as well as how it sounds. You'll want to time your speech again later, once you are more familiar with it and once you've done any further editing. An extemporaneous speech is actually likely to become longer as you practice it. You tend to add embellishments to various points as you become more comfortable with the material. However, this initial run-through as you time your speech will indicate whether you are in the ball park. If you are significantly over the time limits, you know you must cut material somewhere. Perhaps your focus is too broad. If you are significantly under the time limits, try to add material. What points could use additional support?

62. Edit, Edit, Edit

Edit if you exceed the time limits. Don't hesitate to cut material from your speech if, once you time it, you find it runs too long. You know that 20 minutes is the limit for optimum adult attention. You also should know the audience's expectation of length because you followed the advice in Secret #10.

No matter how great you believe your material is, you defeat your goal if you greatly exceed the expected time limit. You will lose your listeners' attention and risk making many of them angry at you. Some will even begin to dislike you. If listeners do not like you, it is difficult to be an effective speaker.

Edit if you can find a better way to make a point. Perhaps the situation has changed and one of your examples is no longer pertinent. Cut it out. Perhaps since you originally put together your speech, you've come across a story that really makes your point. Put it in. Don't be afraid to make a change if it will improve your speech.

63. Anticipate Questions From The Audience

Did you ever wonder how the President does such a good job answering questions thrown at him following his press conferences? Even though he may not know exactly what question Helen Thomas or Sam Donaldson may fire at him, he and his aides know the subjects that are most likely to come up. The President prepares accordingly. So should you!

Once you have prepared your speech, your work is not over. Anticipate the kinds of questions you are likely to be asked. Some may be questions about content asked by a perplexed listener. Others may be questions of motive or intent posed by an antagonistic listener with his own ax to grind. Consider the range of questions you may encounter—including the ones from hostile listeners—and prepare.

For each potential question, consider the strategy of your response. Don't try to memorize answers. At best they will only sound rehearsed, and at worst you'll forget what you tried to memorize. But if you think through a strategy for your response, you'll be prepared, you'll retain your cool composure, and you'll appear polished and competent. It is far easier to think through the strategy of your responses in the secure comfort of your office than to respond on the spot when you are nervous and uncomfortable. Effective speakers try to anticipate everything and leave nothing to chance!

64. *Have Questions Ready To "Throw In The Ring"*

If after the conclusion of your speech you open the floor for questions, and there are none, you may feel it weakens that last impression you leave with your audience. After waiting an appropriate length of time for questions, if there are none, you could wind up by indicating how much you enjoyed the opportunity to speak to them and then move into that second conclusion you are holding in reserve. If it has been a long evening, and you sense that there

> **Success Tip**

Anticipate likely questions, including hostile ones. Prepare two or three questions of your own just in case the audience isn't responsive.

are no questions because everyone wants to get out of there and get home, then this is probably the best course to follow. To lengthen the presentation at a time like this is pointless, and will at best frustrate and at the worst antagonize your audience.

However, are there some questions that you wish someone would ask? Are there questions that you nearly always are asked when you present a speech on this topic? Is there something you wanted to include but didn't feel there was time because you were asked to leave 10 minutes for questions at the end? Part of your preparation might include having two or three questions ready in case the audience isn't responsive. If you ask for questions and there are none, and you believe it is because people are too shy to pose questions or are afraid they will appear foolish, you may pose questions yourself. After a short pause, you could say, "One of the most frequent questions I often get asked is . . . . " After you've answered one question, the audience may loosen up and ask several of their own. At any point—either after you have posed one or two of your own or after the audience has finally made queries—you can conclude with that second closing you were holding in reserve.

Control Fear

TO STAND UP IN FRONT OF A GROUP OF PEOPLE and communicate with them is an opportunity! Yet for many speakers, the very thought fills them with fear and dread rather than excitement and eager anticipation. What is it about addressing an audience of ten or more people that can turn otherwise competent adults into such flustered souls?

Let's take a hard look at this thing called "nervousness." What is it? Where does it come from? And what can one do about it? Ask many speakers what nervousness feels like and the most common responses are: a dry mouth, butterflies in the stomach, weak or shaky knees, a voice that quivers, or wet palms. These are some of the symptoms or manifestations of nervousness. Generally when you have one or more of these feelings, you say you feel nervous, and most speakers wish they could be rid of the feeling. You don't like butterflies in your stomach or knees that feel like jelly. But what created those feelings of anxiety that you want to be rid of?

Let's travel back a few aeons to caveman times. When the caveman saw a saber-toothed tiger in the tall grass, his mind said "Danger!" At this, the adrenal medulla increased the flow of adrenaline and noradrenaline. His heart rate increased, his blood pressure and blood sugar rose, and the blood flow through his muscles increased. The fight-or-flight mechanism was working. If he chose to flee, he could run a bit faster; if he stood his ground to fight, he would fight stronger. It served our species well and our survival was its legacy.

Now fast forward to today. You are about to get up to speak. You look out and see the large audience you are about to address. It's a jungle out there all right, but the enemy isn't a saber-toothed tiger. The enemy is the audience—that group of friendly and supportive people have taken the place of the saber-toothed tiger in your mind! Once your mind sends the message there is danger, your body's defenses go to work to protect you. The adrenaline courses through your veins, but rather than give you the strength to flee or fight better, since you have the need to do neither, it creates all those bodily symptoms you refer to as signs of nervousness.

Nervousness is a symptom of a heightened sensitivity which is needed to perform well. Accept that some nervousness will actually help you perform better. There is no magic pill that will instantly dispel the symptoms of nervousness. But the 13 secrets that follow, taken together, should significantly lessen your feelings of anxiety when you present a speech.

65. Solid Preparation Is Your Best Defense

There is no substitute for being well prepared. The process starts with giving yourself adequate time for preparation, and thoroughly completing each step in the speech "writing" process. From gathering data, selecting the main ideas and supporting materials, formulating an introduction and conclusion, preparing your notes or a manuscript, to practicing—talking through your speech—each step takes time.

If you procrastinate and wait until the night before your speech to begin to prepare, you limit both your effectiveness and your self-confidence. The normal level of nervousness now increases as you realize you've "blown your opportunity." In addition to not having time to adequately prepare your content or become familiar with it, you've neglected the opportunity to investigate the speaking environment. Those gathering butterflies are going to increase when you enter the room where you will be speaking, manuscript in hand—you hadn't the familiarity with the material to be comfortable giving an extemporaneous speech—to find there is no lectern in the room. Every lectern is in use in other rooms!

How much better your speech will be and how much better you will feel if you have taken the time to prepare and digest your material at each step along the way to actually delivering your presentation. Few things are as great a confidence builder as you approach the lectern on the day of your speech as knowing you are prepared.

66. Be Totally Familiar With Your Introduction

Most speakers find they are most nervous immediately prior to and during the first minute—though it may feel like several minutes—of their speeches. Be especially familiar with the introduction of your speech. Once you have gotten through the first minute or two of your speech, you will probably begin to feel more comfortable and confident—especially if this has gone well. Build your confidence as well as your success by knowing your introduction especially well. This is not to suggest that you memorize the introduction, as fears that you may forget what you have memorized or the possibility that you actually do go blank are counter-productive. Whether you are speaking extemporaneously from notes or speaking from a manuscript, know the beginning of your presentation exceedingly well.

67. *Practice Out Loud—Often*

Talk through your speech as many times as you can. Stand up as you deliver your practice presentations and try to approximate those conditions you can control to make them as close to what you will encounter in the actual situation. If you plan to use a lectern, try to rig something similar for your use—even if it is a stack of books or bricks—so you can get used to alternatively looking toward where the audience will be and then at your notes, as well as practice unobtrusively sliding a page of notes across the lectern once you have finished with each page.

 *Success Tip*

If no one is available as a practice audience, try talking to a clock. It has a face, shows movement, and times your speech.

As you practice, the most important thing is that you actually talk through the speech. How many people, if any, are listening is not important. There may be no one in your practice audience or you may speak in front of your child, your spouse, or a friend. If no one is readily available to pose as an audience for your practice sessions, I often suggest that speakers talk to a clock. It has a face, it may show more movement than some listeners, and it provides an opportunity to time your speech.

If you plan to present an extemporaneous speech, practice establishing as much eye contact as possible with the area where the audience will be seated during your actual presentation. Talk to this audience area, sweeping the room with your eyes while stopping to establish eye contact with various items in the room—as you will establish eye contact with listeners during your actual presentation. As you near the end of your comments about the point you are making, but before you actually finish the thought you are on, look at your notes to determine the next point you will cover. Look back at your audience as you complete your present thought and then transition smoothly to your next point.

During your practice sessions you will be able to determine whether your notes are sufficient to trigger each idea in your mind as you talk through your speech. If you have too many notes—which is likely—pare them down. Remember, the fewer notes you take to the lectern the better, as long as the notes are sufficient to trigger the ideas you want to present. If your notes are too few, add what you need at the appropriate place. If you have left plenty of space as suggested in Secret #59, you should be able to insert a word or phrase and still have lots of blank space so you can easily find your place when you glance at your notes. Or perhaps you don't need to add anything but, rather, underline a thought with a red pen or highlight with a felt-tipped marker.

If you have prepared a manuscript speech, you, too, need to talk through the speech out loud. You learn to pace at a comfortable rate for your listeners, you become so familiar with your speech that you can establish frequent eye contact with your listeners, you become familiar with where ideas fall on the page. You also can make use of red pens to underline or felt-tipped markers to highlight ideas you want to stress or mark a place you need to be able to find more easily.

No matter what your delivery format, use these practice sessions to acquire confidence by gaining familiarity with your material and the notes or manuscript you have constructed. Be sure you can pronounce all words you may use, and time your speech to assure that you will be within the time limits.

68. Record Your Speech

Practice talking through your speech a few times before you record it. You will be your own harshest critic, so give yourself a chance to practice first. After you have talked through your speech a few times, videotape a practice session if you can. But if videotaping is not readily accessible, an audiotape can yield a lot of information. Watch or listen to your tape and make notes of things you want to modify. Practice a few more times without taping, trying to incorporate changes in the areas you wanted to modify. Then record yourself again. You should notice improvements in the targeted areas. Don't allow your internal critic to batter your self-image. None of us is ever satisfied with how we see or hear ourselves. Allow your internal coach to take over as you view or listen to the tapes. Your internal coach will help you identify what you can modify in order to make a better presentation. These positive attempts at behavior modification are what is needed as you refine and polish your presentation.

69. Practice Mentally

Although practice by delivering your speech out loud is important, you can supplement these practice sessions by talking through the speech silently to yourself. If you have a few minutes during your lunch break or while riding the bus or train to work, it is possible to look at your notes and, as you focus on each "trigger" on your notes, mentally think through the points you wish to make. This process is a useful way to increase your comfort level for those short speeches you give. If you present lengthy speeches—20 minutes or longer—you may not have the time to actually talk through the speech as many times as you would like. For these longer speeches the mental practice will take on greater importance.

70. Focus On Ideas—Not Exact Phrases (Extemporaneous Delivery)

If you have selected an extemporaneous delivery, remember as you practice—as well as when you actually deliver the speech—that you are not trying to say the same thing in the same way each time you present it. That would be memorization. Your goal is to use your notes to trigger in your mind the ideas you want to present in the order you have pre-determined. Once that idea has been triggered, try to the convey the idea to your listeners in the words that come to you. You may find you use some phrases almost each and every time you talk through your speech, but other ideas may be phrased some-what differently from one practice to another. This is as it should be. Don't feel bound by one way of communicating an idea. Don't be alarmed that you find yourself communicating your ideas in different ways; this is the way it should be. You should focus on communicating your ideas—not an exact phraseology. Let go of the idea that you have to say the same thing in the same way each time.

 **Success Tip**

Focus on communicating your ideas—not exact words or phrases. Your notes should trigger these ideas.

If you will do this, you need never be afraid of forgetting your speech. There is nothing to forget. Your notes will trigger in your mind the ideas you have selected to present. Since it is the ideas and not an exact way of phrasing them that you wish to convey, go with what comes to your mind at the time.

71. Concentrate On Your Message Rather Than On Yourself

Concentrate on your message and your goal—to convey that message to your listeners. Put all of your energy into this mission and you will not have time to think about yourself. It is easier said than done, but it is a powerful secret of effective speakers. Nervousness comes, in part, from focusing one's attention on the internal question, "How am I doing?" If your focus is on **yourself** and how **you** are doing, how **you** look, how **you** sound, what the audience thinks about **you**, your energy is misplaced. Focus instead on your message. You believe in it. You believe it is important to your listeners. Put your focus where it should be—on your message and your listeners —and before you know it, you will realize you don't feel nervous.

Several years ago I was sharing a day's presentation with my husband and colleague in what was at the time one of the CIA's seminar rooms in Rosslyn, Virginia. The building was located not far from the flight path taken by planes as they flew along the Potomac River on their approach to Reagan National Airport. Ron addressed the group of about 50 soon-to-be retired government employees for the morning session. I was seated at the back of the room with the participants. At the morning break, I mentioned to Ron that when the planes flew overhead it was a bit hard to hear him at the back of the room, and suggested that he try to project his voice a bit more—especially when the planes flew overhead. He indicated he had not heard any planes at all, but he would try to project better.

When the afternoon session began, it was Ron's turn to sit in the audience. I presented the material that I had prepared for my part of the program. At the end of the day, after the participants had left, I chatted with Ron and the program director. I commented that the wind direction must have changed by the afternoon since the planes had no longer been flying overhead. They looked at me strangely, then one said, "The planes were still flying over during the entire afternoon."

I was so involved with my message and my audience —with my entire attention focused on them—that I had not heard the planes during the afternoon session while I was speaking, even though I had been very aware of them during the morning when I was a member of the audience. It explained why Ron had been oblivious to them while he was speaking in the morning.

Ask people what they fear most about giving a speech and they often respond, "I am afraid I will make a fool of myself in front of my boss (or "peers," "subordinates," or "friends"). Their fear is usually not of failing to communicate a message, but a fear of appearing inadequate! Concentrate on the message you want to communicate and you will soon forget about yourself. Effective speakers believe in the message they present and focus on imparting that message to their listeners.

72. Nervousness Connects You To The Human Race

Everyone experiences some nervousness making presentations— the difference is one of degree. The degree of a speaker's apprehension varies according to many factors: one's individual personality, amount of preparation, and amount of public speaking experience account for the most variation of nervousness experienced by various speakers. The inexperienced speaker may anticipate each speech with a great deal of nervous apprehension. An experienced speaker will usually feel more at ease—at least with audiences and situations that are familiar. But even an experienced speaker may find that the old feelings of nervousness return if he is asked to make a presentation to an audience that is quite different than those he is accustomed to addressing.

Understanding that feeling some degree of nervousness is common to everyone should help you accept these feelings as a normal part of being human. Recognize, too, that you are in good company. Many famous and accomplished individuals from U.S. presidents to award-winning actors and actresses admit to always having experienced some degree of apprehension prior to going before an audience. Helen Hayes, Johnny Carson, Carol Burnett, Merv Griffin, Joan Rivers, Liza Minnelli, Sidney Poitier, and Christopher Reeves have all talked publicly about their continuing efforts to deal with nervousness. So you get nervous before presenting a speech? You are in good company!

73. Remember: You Appear Much More Confident Than You Feel

So your hands are shaking and your knees wobbling and you are sure your audience can see it. You can feel your voice trembling and you are certain your listeners can hear it. You are terrified and your audience can't help but be aware of it. Right? Probably not! Time after time participants in my seminars sit down at the end of their speech, breathe a sigh of relief, and say how nervous they were. They are sure we were all aware of it—even sitting there feeling sorry for them as we listened because we, the audience, were so acutely aware of their nervousness. The truth? Almost always, their delivery showed no overt signs of the nervousness they felt. Even when they have shared with the rest of the group for three days how nervous they get when making a presentation, usually the only clue we have is their protestations to that fact.

Even when we—the other participants as well as myself—tell them how self-assured and professional they appeared, they assure us how nervous they felt. Do we believe them? Of course we do. But what they need to understand is that what they are feeling does not show. It is not apparent to the audience. If they did not tell us, we would not know. Most of us have learned to hide our feelings of nervousness and are quite good at it! Even after speakers have seen their presentations on video-tape, they still try to convince us that they really did feel nervous.

So remember: for most speakers the nervousness that you feel will not show. Let this knowledge build your confidence. And since you want your presentation to be as professional and polished as possible, don't spoil your secret by telling everyone either before or after your speech how nervous you felt. Accept compliments graciously.

74. Breathe Deeply From Your Diaphragm

Any of you who have played a wind instrument or sung in a choir will know about your diaphragm and how to breathe from your diaphragm. For those of you who do not, take one of your hands and make a fist. Center that fist at your midsection with the thumb at or slightly below your navel. Hold your fist still, and try to thrust your fist outward using outward pressure from the muscle you should find behind or slightly below your navel.

A deep breath that starts from the diaphragm will counter **some** of the feelings of nervousness being produced by the increased adrenaline. A deep breath before you leave your seat, another as you approach the lectern, and yet another just before you begin to speak will have a calming effect.

75. Channel Your Adrenaline

You know now that the increased adrenaline is your body's defense mechanism to help you in difficult situations. Even though it may seem to be your enemy in the 21st century when you have no need to battle saber-toothed tigers, adrenaline is still your ally. Rather than fight it, put that extra energy into your presentation. Use the adrenaline rush to generate and sustain the enthusiasm that will make you a dynamic speaker. That adrenaline will also keep you alert and heighten your ability to think on your feet.

Effective speakers are dynamic speakers. Just ask Michael Dukakis, Bob Dole, or Al Gore what a lack of dynamism can do to thwart reaching one's goal.

76. Dress For The Occasion: Dress To Build Confidence

Before you ever open your mouth to speak, your listeners have already begun to form impressions about you. Whether you are competent, whether you are trustworthy, whether you are likeable—before you say a word, these impressions are being formed. Like it or not, initially others do judge us based on our appearance. So select your attire based, in part, on the messages you wish to convey to your audience. Is it your goal to appear authoritative and powerful? Trustworthy? Likeable?

Two components of credibility—the speaker's expertise and his trustworthiness—were introduced in Secret #43. The third component—the speaker's dynamism—will be the focus of Secret #84. The attire you select can enhance or detract from any or all of these aspects of your credibility. As a result of the analysis of your audience, the situation, and how you, the speaker, are likely to be viewed—Secrets #4 through #7—you can determine how to best select your clothing to help you achieve your goal.

In some situations your primary goal will be to convey non-verbal messages that say you are competent and in control. Your goal when selecting your attire will be to chose clothing that enhances your look of expertise, authority, and power to the maximum. If you are a male, your most powerful look is a suit—a dark gray or a dark blue—paired with a white long-sleeved shirt and a tie. If you are female, a suit is also your most powerful look, and traditional colors of dark gray or navy work best.

> **Caution!**

Even before you open your mouth to speak, your audience has already formed impressions about you based upon your appearance.

However, women have leeway with the selection of other dark colors such as maroon which may neither detract or add to their power look. But though you will choose to enhance the credibility of your message with the careful selection of your attire, it is not only the image of expertise you may wish to accentuate. Perhaps you are as concerned with how trustworthy you appear to your listeners. Speakers—both men and women—will find a medium blue or navy suit paired with a white shirt or blouse will enhance the degree of trust felt by their audience.

In other situations you may choose to deemphasize a look of power so as to appear less powerful or intimidating to an audience. Many Federal Government employees who participate in my seminars indicate that when they leave Washington, D.C. to visit their agency's regional offices, they often choose to dress in clothing that says "professional" but does not scream "powerful." They are already perceived as an outsider in the regional offices and they believe they can gain better cooperation when they do not set themselves apart greatly from the audience they are addressing. A man may elect to wear a suit in a color that conveys less authority or may choose slacks, sport coat and tie. Either option says "professional" but "less powerful." A woman may select a suit in colors that convey less power or wear a base of the one color—a navy skirt and blouse—with a jacket in either a contrasting color or a plaid that picks up the color of the base.

There may be times when you have other specialized goals. For example, the color yellow conveys messages of "like me" and "I'm not threatening." Is that why Elizabeth Dole selected a yellow suit for the speech she presented to the Republican National Convention which nominated her husband for the Presidency? The suit conveyed "professional"—as did her polished speech. But the color conveyed to those who might fear a "co-president" that she would not be a threat, as did her delivery style—made less formal as she left the platform and podium to walk on the convention floor among the audience.

Whatever your apparel decisions, analyze your choices and your reasons carefully. You have spent a lot of time preparing your speech. Select attire that conveys nonverbal messages that further your goal.

As you analyzed the speaking situation, did you consider physical elements of the place where you will present your speech? Will you be on a stage? Will bright lights be focused on you? Will you be speaking in a dimly lit room or auditorium? Will you be behind a lectern? If you speak in a dimly lit room, a dark suit may need a light or bright accent—in the necktie or scarf—to bring you to life. Some women report choosing to wear a red suit or jacket when presenting a speech because they believe the color helps keep listeners' attention focused on them. However, if you will be bathed in bright lighting, you might choose to tone down a red jacket or accessories. If you will be on a high platform or stage, and especially if there's no lectern, be very careful about the length of your skirt!

Matt Lauer, co-host of the *Today Show*, was interviewed one evening on *Larry King Live* shortly after moving into his new role. Among other questions, Larry asked Matt whether his attire had changed since he assumed the role of hosting the show. Matt responded that he did not think his attire had changed much since the days he was televising the news, but that perhaps he was dressing a bit less casually these days. He explained that now, as host, he wore a suit everyday. Because of fast breaking news, he might unexpectedly be thrust in the position of interviewing a high level official or head of state. A suit provides the visual credibility the audience expects in such a situation and no doubt would add to his own self-confidence as well.

By dressing to fit the occasion and your goals, you will build your self-confidence. Knowing you "look the part" will help you "act the part" of a confident, poised presenter. Effective speakers earn audience good-will and trust and are viewed as having expertise based initially on how they look. The speaker can then build on this positive start with a well prepared and focused message.

77. "Psych" Yourself Into Readiness

Do you remember the song from *The King and I* where Anna counsels her son to *"Whistle A Happy Tune"*? She tells him if he'll whistle whenever he feels afraid, he'll not only fool others—he'll fool himself as well! Psychologists tell us that our minds can only hold one thought at a time. Are you going to let your "internal critic" take over and hold thoughts of fear and failure in your mind? Or will you allow your "internal coach" to take the lead and fill your mind with thoughts of confidence and success?

Visualize the role you want to play—one of confidence and self-assurance—and act the part. Approach the lectern with a purposeful and confident stride; stand erect behind the lectern with your head held high and your shoulders square and back straight; project your voice with an air of confidence; convey your conviction and enthusiasm in your manner and the projection of your voice. These actions form part of the basis for the next section which deals with commanding the attention of your audience. But these behaviors are equally important to your feelings of self-confidence as you command your body to behave in ways consistent with your goal of appearing—as well as being—self-assured. Fill your mind with confident, positive thoughts. Carry your body as if you feel confident and positive, and you can manage to both look and feel confident and positive.

78. Seek Help—If Needed

Most of you will find that following the preceding 13 "secrets" will significantly lessen your fear of public speaking. By following the advice to prepare well and to focus on ideas rather than exact phrases, you will build confidence and be able to present your speeches well. In addition, secret 100, "Seek and Accept Opportunities to Speak" serves many purposes, and helping speakers build confidence is one of them. The more positive experiences you have, the more comfortable you will feel when you think about a presentation you are about to make. Remember, if you feel confident and don't tell yourself there is a danger out there—you know, the saber-toothed tiger—you won't feel the many effects of that extra adrenalin rushing through your body.

Remember that some feelings of nervousness are normal and will even help you make a better presentation as your heightened state of attention keeps you mentally alert. However, there are some people who experience more than the normal degree of nervousness and who may need special assistance to help them overcome their fears. How do you know whether your nervousness is in the "normal fear" or "greater than normal fear" range? The following guideline may help you determine whether you should seek additional help. If you experience various signs of nervousness such as butterflies in your stomach, a dry mouth, a feeling of slightly wobbly knees or shaking hands, or you are sure your voice is going to quiver or your face be flushed, but when the time comes to get up and present your speech you are able to do it, you are probably experiencing nervousness the same way most all of us do. You may even find that you do not sleep as well as usual the night before a presentation, but you do sleep.

If, however, you simply **cannot**—no matter how much you think you should, and even though you are well prepared—get up and give the speech, you probably can benefit from special assistance. You may be experiencing more than the usual communication apprehension. If you believe you need special assistance I recommend you first get a copy of ***Triumph Over Fear*** by Jerilyn Ross. Reading this book may give you all the help you need to deal with your heightened apprehension. In addition, there is a wonderful resource section at the end of the book that suggests additional reading on the subject as well as a listing of health professionals, organized by state, who offer one-on-one assistance or group counseling. Some clinics located in Canada are also listed. Jerilyn Ross operates The Ross Center for Anxiety and Related Disorders in Washington, DC. Call 800-545-7367 or locally 202-363-1010. The local number should be answered by a person; you are likely to get a recording if you call the 800 number. You can also contact the center by email at: Jerilyn@rosscenter.com. They have a website you may wish to visit: www.rosscenter.com

Command Attention: Your Demeanor Conveys Authority

YOU'VE HEAD THE ADAGE, "YOU NEVER GET A second chance to make a first impression." When you face an audience make it a positive first impression. Before you say a word your listeners are forming impressions of you—whether you seem competent, trustworthy, likable. From how you dress, how you approach the lectern, how you project your voice, the audience is making judgments about you based on many non-verbal cues.

You begin to command attention as you step up to the lectern with a confident, purposeful demeanor; an enthusiastic walk, head held high with shoulders back and a confident facial expression. You command attention as you stand erect behind the lectern, weight evenly distributed on both feet. You command attention as you look out at your audience and pause before you speak. And when you do speak, you command attention in the way you project your voice and convey dynamism. Let's look at these delivery factors that convey your credibility, competence, and professionalism and in so doing, command attention from your audience. You want to appear in control, confident, credible, and dynamic.

79. Approach The Lectern With Confidence

What do you, as a listener, think when you see a speaker step up to the front of the room with a strong purposeful stride, shoulders back and head held high, and with a determined, confident demeanor? Contrast that speaker with one who takes small, tentative steps toward the lectern, and who walks with shoulders slumped and a fearful expression on his face. You must begin to command attention by the very manner in which you step up to the lectern to present your speech.

This is the time to *"Whistle A Happy Tune"*—so to speak. Even if your knees feel like jelly, your outward demeanor must convey a confident person who is in control and really anxious to share your message with this audience. As the lyrics say, as you engage in non-verbal behaviors to fool the audience, a bonus benefit is that the confident manner you project to the listeners will make you feel more confident as well.

The audience will grant far greater credibility and hence attention to the speaker whose demeanor exudes confidence than to the speaker whose body language conveys meekness and a lack of confidence. So leave your seat with a confident, enthusiastic gait, body carriage, and facial expression, and step up to the lectern with a purposeful demeanor that conveys your pleasure at the opportunity to address this group.

80. Get Set Before You Speak

Have you ever seen a speaker who began talking before he got to the front of the room, let alone behind the lectern? Or have you observed a speaker who got to the lectern and started speaking as he hastily arranged his notes? These are not the behaviors of polished speakers.

If you are using notes or a manuscript, walk to the lectern carrying the papers in the hand that will be the less visible to the audience. You are not trying to hide your notes, but neither do you need to flaunt them. By carrying notes in the hand that is away from the audience, your notes will be less obtrusive and many listeners will not even notice them.

When you reach the front of the room, position yourself behind the lectern. Arrange your notes—the pages should already be in proper order—take a deep breath, look out at your audience, and pause before you begin. When you look out at your audience, it is a signal that you are about to begin. At this point the audience chatter should diminish, although there will be audible sounds as listeners position themselves in their chairs to give atten-

> *Success Tip*

As you approach the lectern, carry your notes or manuscript in the hand less visible to the audience.

tion to your message. The pause before you speak serves three purposes. First, it gives time for the audience chatter to die down. Second, it gives you a moment to collect your thoughts, get your first sentence clear in your head, take another deep breath if you need one, and remember how glad you are to have this opportunity to present an important message to this audience. Third, the pause is a sign of a polished, confident speaker!

81. Stand Erect Behind The Lectern

Have you ever seen a speaker lean all over the lectern, propping himself up as if without the lectern to hold his weight, he would surely not be able to stand? To lean on the lectern conveys an informality as well as a lack of strength and forcefulness that fails to command attention. As you begin your speech, either stand erect behind the lectern or if you chose not to use the lectern, move away from it altogether.

It is permissible to rest a hand on the side of the lectern closest to you, the speaker, if that makes you feel comfortable. Try not to grasp the lectern and hold on for dear life. Even if the audience cannot see this, you limit the likelihood that you will use that hand in natural gestures. Another danger if you grasp the lectern is that you start "playing" with the lectern. I recall one speaker who, in his nervousness, "outlined" the lectern through most of his speech. He started with each hand at the top corners of the lectern nearest to him. he moved his hands in a parallel motion up the top sides of the lectern till he reached the top corners facing the audience. At this point his hands moved toward each other until they met in the center top of the lectern. Next his hands retraced their motion from the center back toward the outside top corners. He then proceeded to move both hands down the outside edges of the lectern facing the audience until they reached the bottom, at which point he began to repeat the various tracing steps. These hand tracings were an outlet for his nervousness, and he was totally unaware of what he was doing. But the audience was intent on where the hands would move next! Did he have the audience's attention? Yes, but the audience was paying far less attention to what the speaker was saying than what he was doing. This distraction was interfering with communication of the message.

Your goal is not to attract attention, but to command attention. Use the lectern to hold your notes, but not to hold you!

82. Distribute Your Weight Evenly On Both Feet

We have all seen the speaker who teeters from side to side or front to back as he speaks. This, too, can quickly become a distraction to the audience. Once a behavior becomes so pronounced that the listeners' attention is focused on the behavior, rather than the message, it has become a negative. Even if a speaker does not teeter, with most of his weight on one foot, a speaker presents an informal stance. Women standing with their weight on one foot often will dangle their other shoe—this behavior made more likely for women because a pump will slip off a foot more easily than a laced wing-tip!

Standing with your weight evenly distributed on both feet forces you to stand taller and makes you appear in control and hence confident. Your stance gives added weight to the importance of your message and adds strength to your perceived credibility.

83. Project Your Voice: Speak With Authority

You might be surprised how many speakers—both men and women—simply don't project their voice well enough to be easily heard. Yes, there are microphones—the subject of Secret #97—but microphones are not always available and often do not work well when they are provided. But even if you use a microphone, you want to come across as confident rather than tentative, so the habit of voice projection is a crucial one to build. You need to project your voice to be **heard**, to **maintain interest**, and to be **perceived as credible**.

You need to project your voice well enough to be heard by everyone in your audience. You must not only be able to be heard, but to be easily heard. If your listeners can hear you, but must strain to hear you, most will soon take a mental exit. It is hard work to constantly strain to hear a speaker. So after a few minutes of working hard at hearing the speaker, most listeners will decide it is too great an effort, give up, and begin thinking of other things—from the project they are working on at the office to what they will do during the coming weekend! For your speech to be effective—to inform or persuade your listeners—they have to hear your message.

Beyond being heard, critical though this is, voice projection is necessary to build the credibility of the speaker. The speaker who speaks with a low volume is perceived as having less status, power, expertise, and dynamism than the speaker who projects well. If you are shorter than average, appear youthful, or are female, it especially behooves you to project your voice adequately to establish your credibility and convey your authority from the very beginning of your presentation. Women can project their voices as well as men; so don't buy into the notion that you can't project adequately because you are female. You want the audience to view you as being knowledgeable? You want the audience to view you as an authority? You want the audience to believe you are committed to your cause or view? **Project your voice!**

If you don't, at present, project your voice well—you know or have been told that you are difficult to hear—you will initially have to project more than what you think is necessary. In other words, if what feels comfortable to you now is not enough, in order to gain appropriate vocal projection you will have to project more than you do at present. That may seem like too much to you at first. Fear not, I have yet to hear a speaker who projects too much. It is indeed a rarity if it happens at all! As you breathe from your diaphragm, you will gain the force for vocal projection from your diaphragm—not your vocal cords. So don't strain your vocal cords; instead, start the breath with your diaphragm and let it propel your voice beyond the last row of the audience. Even if you are using a microphone you need to project your voice. That projection adds to your dynamism and, in the process, to your credibility.

The credibility of the message rises in proportion to the audience's regard for the person bearing it. So, speak with the authority of a person who is in control, in charge, in command. Project your voice, and as you build your credibility your listeners will be more receptive to your ideas.

84. Convey Dynamism

Dynamism is that excitement, that enthusiasm from the speaker that conveys authority as well as conviction to the listeners. Its result is a liveliness that puts a sparkle in your eyes, animation on your face, a forcefulness in your voice and says to your audience, "I really believe this. So you should too." Real feelings light up your voice and face. I don't suggest you try to fake enthusiasm but, rather, that you select speaking goals you truly believe in and then let that natural enthusiasm show.

If you are a low-keyed person by nature, it would behoove you to practice displaying a greater degree of facial expression and gestures and projecting greater vocal forcefulness. Avoid what I refer to as the "Tsongas, Dukakis, Dole and Gore syndrome." All were men of vision, experience, and expertise, but each one's lack of dynamism was a major factor in his failure to attain the highest office in the country—President of the United States.

85. Conclude; then Leave the Lectern With Confidence

Your speech isn't really over until you get back in your car to drive home! No exaggerated sighs of relief at the close; no rolling of your eyes as if to say, "Thank heavens, that's over" as you start to walk back to your seat; no hunching of your shoulders as if to suggest the weight of the world has just been lifted! A professional would never do any of these things, and you want to develop into a professional and polished speaker.

So, take pride in the speech you have just presented. Retain that assured demeanor as you conclude, leave the lectern, and return to your seat still exuding confidence. If you talk with audience members at the end of the program, don't share with them all the little things that went wrong or demean your presentation in any way. If there were elements of your presentation that you wish had gone better, resolve to work harder on those aspects of your presentation for the next speech. For now, accept graciously any compliments listeners may offer and be ready to answer questions they may have.

Sharpen Your Delivery

IF THE FIRST THING THE AUDIENCE NOTICES AND responds to is the speaker's appearance, the second thing is the speaker's delivery. A speaker who is easy to listen to can attract and maintain listeners' attention. It is a bit like the chicken and egg dilemma, as through the centuries rhetoricians have debated which is the more important—the speech content or its delivery. Without good delivery the message gets lost; but without meaningful content there is no message. But there is little doubt a speaker with good delivery skills has a much better chance of focusing and maintaining audience attention on the message than does the speaker with poor delivery.

You can sharpen your delivery skills with practice. Because you may not always be aware of behaviors you engage in while speaking, you will need feedback. You can get feedback from a friend or family member who listens to your practice session or from an audio or videotape playback. With an audiotape playback you will miss visual aspects of your delivery: facial expression, eye contact with listeners, and use of gestures and physical movement. But you will be able to assess your pace, your pauses—both vocalized and silent pauses—your variety of vocal inflection, as well as your vocal projection.

Many of the shortcomings you may notice as you watch and listen to your delivery on videotape are behaviors you likely exhibit in other settings as well—not just presenting a speech. This actually works to your advantage. It means that you can work on modifying behaviors you wish to change in your everyday settings. See Secret #88. If your diction is unclear, work on improving it everyday. If you use lots of fillers and vocalized pauses, minimize their use in your daily conversations and it will carry over to your formal presentations.

86. *Speak Clearly*

Strive for clear diction and the correct pronunciation of every word you utter. With clear diction and proper pronunciation, your message will be more easily understood by listeners. You, the speaker, will be perceived as more credible and powerful.

Diction is the production of sounds. Diction may be sloppy and slovenly or crisp and professional. Sloppy diction is exhibited when someone drops the "ing" sounds at the end of words such as saying "goin" rather than "going" or when one doesn't clearly articulate such as saying "Adlanta" rather than "Atlanta." Sloppy diction creates the impression that the speaker is of a lower level of education, social standing, and position, and hence lowers his credibility in the minds of the listeners.

Pronunciation is how you deliver words—where the accent falls as well as the pronunciation of sounds. Some elements of pronunciation vary with geographical region. In parts of New England, "idea" becomes "idear" or "car" sounds like "cah."

Know that as you move from one geographical area to another, your speech patterns may be distracting to an audience or may actually diminish or enhance your credibility. Speech patterns from the Boston area may be perceived as erudite in other areas of the country, whereas speech patterns from other regions may lower the perceived credibility of the speaker. Again, having analyzed your audience and yourself as the speaker to this audience, you should be alert to how your regional patterns of speech will affect their perception of you and your message. The language patterns of the areas skirting the great lakes—Chicago, Cleveland, Erie, Buffalo—have long been considered to be the most dialect free or the most representative of standard American speech. Years ago, would-be radio announcers often went or were sent to these cities to "lose" their accents!

Correct pronunciation means checking the pronunciation of any unfamiliar words—including the names of any places or persons. The wrong pronunciation will make you appear less knowledgeable and well informed, and at worst, may actually offend listen-

 **Caution!**

Sloppy diction communicates negative messages to an audience—the speaker is poorly educated and lower class. It damages the speaker's credibility.

ers. Enhance your polish and professional demeanor. Make a habit of using clear diction in your day-to-day communication and you will carry it automatically into your public speaking. Be sure you know the correct pronunciation and you will be perceived as a more credible and more powerful speaker.

87. *Vary Your Pace: Pace For Your Listeners*

Do you have a tendency to speak at one rate throughout your entire speech? When you feel nervous do you speak rapidly? Do you speak so slowly that people want to finish your sentences for you? Your pace is the rate—how rapidly or slowly—at which you articulate words.

Ideally your speaking rate should be comfortable for your listeners. Too fast, and it is difficult for your listeners to follow your message. It is hard work to keep up with a speaker whose pace is too rapid, and after working at following your meaning for a while, many listeners will begin to daydream. Too rapid a pace and your listeners may take a mental exit. Slow the pace too much and a speech becomes deadly dull and you also lose your listeners. To find out if your pace is a comfortable one for listeners, ask a couple of people to listen to you rehearse and get honest feedback from them. Alternatively, listen to the tape of your practice session.

Strive for a comfortable pace for your listeners, but vary the pace slightly if your speech is a long one. You can slow a bit to emphasize a point and then pick it back up to that comfortable listening rate. Varying your pace will help keep listeners focused on your message. A pace that is neither too fast nor too slow will also build your credibility with the audience. A too rapid rate makes a speaker sound frightened, but a pace that is comfortable to listen to conveys that the speaker is confident.

88. *Pause Often*

Don't be afraid of silent pauses. Silent pauses give you, the speaker, a chance to collect your thoughts—both before you begin your speech and throughout your delivery. Silent pauses provide an opportunity for your audience to listen better—to keep up with your message and to process the message. Silent pauses should be used after questions are posed to the audience. They give the listeners time to respond to themselves. Pauses can be used as a transition between points, and are an aid when the speaker wishes to provide emphasis for a point. Silent pauses can actually build expectation on the part of the listeners. The speaker needs pauses. Pauses provide an opportunity for the speaker to consider what he will say next as well as a chance to breathe. The listeners need pauses. Many inexperienced speakers talk too fast and don't pause often enough for the audience to listen comfortably. If a too rapid speaking rate is combined with a lack of pauses, the problem for listeners is intensified. Listeners need pauses, otherwise listening becomes hard work. If one tires of working so hard at listening, they will just tune the speaker out.

Have you just walked up to the lectern, arranged your notes, taken a deep breath, and looked out at your audience? Pause before you begin to speak. Have you just asked your listeners a rhetorical question? Pause immediately following the question. Let the question sink in. Allow the listeners time to respond with an answer internally. If you pose the question and then rush on, you have not only negated the positive

> **Success Tip**

Both the speaker and the audience need pauses—the speaker to catch his breath and the audience to listen intently.

effect of involving your listeners as they answer the question to themselves, you have also left them feeling frustrated—though they may not fully understand why they feel as they do. Have you just made a point you wish to emphasize? Pause. You pause both to let the point fully sink in as well as to let the audience know this is important. Do you wish to make a transition between major points in your speech? Pause. The pause will help your listeners shift their attention with you.

Make a habit of pausing—in silence—frequently as you speak. Pause to gather your thoughts, pause to allow listeners to digest your meaning, pause for transition, pause for emphasis, pause to allow time for listeners to internally answer a question. Finally, pause to add to your effectiveness as a speaker.

89. Limit Use Of Vocalized Pauses & Fillers

Just as silent pauses are your friend, vocalized pauses are your enemy. A vocalized pause is space the speaker fills with "ah" or "and ah." A filler refers to filling space with "like" or "you know." Most of us will occasionally use a vocalized pause or a filler. An occasional vocalized pause in an extemporaneous speech is not a problem. It becomes a problem for a speaker when he does it with such frequency that it calls attention to itself. Once listeners become focused on the vocalized pauses, they have lost sight of the message. I have heard speakers make such frequent use of vocalized pauses that audience members started keeping track by making marks on a piece of paper each time the speaker said another "ah"! With audience attention focused on how many times the speaker would say "and ah," the message received scant attention.

So how do you know if you sprinkle your speech with too many vocalized pauses? How do you limit their use if you do find you utter more than your share of vocalized pauses? First, listen to either a video or audio recorded tape of your practice speech. You should be able to hear if you excessively engage in vocalized pauses. Second, ask others to listen to the tape as well. If their assessment is that you could improve your delivery by limiting your use of vocalized pauses and fillers, then try the behavior modification steps that follow.

1. **You identify a behavior you wish to change**. In this case you want to "limit vocalized pauses."

2. **You make a commitment to yourself to change the behavior**. If you are really committed to the change, this process will work for you. But **you** have to want to change. Just the fact that someone else wants you to change is not enough.

3. **You must become aware that you have engaged in the behavior** each time you have done it. This happens after the fact, but nonetheless you must be aware you have "done it again." You may wish to enlist the aid of another person(s) to let you know you have done it—perhaps a friend at the office or/and a spouse at home. This person should gently remind you that you have just said "ah" again—or whatever the thing is you are doing and wish to change.

4. As time goes by, **you will be aware of what you are saying as you are doing it**. Because you become aware in the midst of saying it, you will not be able to modify it at this point, but your awareness of the behavior is coming about earlier in your speaking.

5. As more time goes by, **you will be aware you are about to say the thing you want to change**. At this point, with the earlier awareness, you can modify what you are about to do. For example, pause with silence rather than filling the pause with sound.

6. With more time, **the new behavior will have replaced the old** and will come as naturally to you as the initial behavior once did. You will no longer have to think about what you are doing. It will now be your normal behavior—both in one-on-one situations and public speaking.

I have seen these behavior modification steps work wonders with many speakers—allowing them to limit their use of vocalized pauses in both one-to-one and public speaking settings. Normally it will take some time—perhaps a few weeks to effect a significant change. But I have seen one speaker make the metamorphosis from using an average of three to four vocalized pauses per sentence—the worst I have ever encountered—to an average of only one vocalized pause in several sentences within a one-week period. I suspect that speaker was especially dedicated to making the modification.

This method is successful at modifying behavior because the behavior can be worked on in settings where interactions take place on a daily basis—talking with co-workers at the office or interacting with a small group of friends at lunch. Individuals who use excessive vocalized pauses when delivering speeches also use excessive vocalized pauses as they interact with others on a daily basis. Hence, if a behavior can be modified in daily interactions, it will carry over to the public speaking setting. Effective speakers make frequent use of silent pauses but limit their use of vocalized pauses.

90. *Vary Your Inflection*

The opposite of a speaker with a variety of vocal inflection is one who speaks in a monotone. A presentation delivered in a monotone is flat and uninteresting to listen to. Variety of vocal inflection makes a delivery easier on the audience and results in better attention and understanding. Because a variety of inflection is one component of a dynamic delivery, a variety of inflection will help the speaker be perceived as being more dynamic. This in turn enhances the speaker's credibility.

Loosen up so that your facial expression is more lively. This will help you inject vocal variety into your presentations. With greater facial expression will come greater inflection.

91. Look At Everyone Frequently

We all know that good eye contact is important for speakers to achieve and maintain. So important, in fact, that you have probably heard people suggest ploys for speakers to use to trick listeners into thinking the speaker is looking at them. A well-intentioned person may tell a novice speaker to look just above the heads of the audience and the listeners will think the speaker is looking at them. Reject this and all similar advice. To begin with, in all but a large auditorium setting with house lights down and a well lighted stage, the audience will know immediately if you are looking over their heads rather than at them. You won't fool anyone.

Look at your listeners as individuals—after all that is what they are—rather than as one large aggregate. Let your eyes sweep the room slowly. Let your eyes stop from time to time on various individuals until your eyes actually "lock" with theirs. Then continue repeating this process until you have "connected" with more of the listeners. With a small audience of 25-30 people, you should be able to make this connect at least once with each member of the audience. With a very large audience, connect with as many of the listeners as you can. You are establishing a bond with your listeners, and they feel you relating directly to each of them.

Good eye contact with your listeners is maintained first by being thoroughly familiar with your speech and having practiced its delivery from your notes (or manuscript) so that you spend only a small proportion of your time glancing down at your notes. Most of the time you are heads-up. In addition, as you look out at your audience you engage them as individuals rather than viewing them as a mass of people—a single entity—sitting in front of you. At the outset, when you are most likely to be the most nervous, connect with the positive, friendly faces in your audience. As you become more comfortable, try to make the visual connection with other listeners as well.

Through your eye contact your listeners will find it easier to pay attention to your message because they have a "connect" with the messenger. Your listeners will be more receptive to your persuasive appeals because you have related to them as individuals. You will be able to note and assess the non-verbal messages from your listeners and adapt your message to what you believe they need. Engage your listeners by establishing frequent eye contact with as many of them as possible.

92. *Use Movement To Maintain Attention*

Five pictures are hanging on the wall—one falls. Which has your attention? Movement is an attention getter. Some movement, from one spot to another, will help keep the attention of your listeners. It takes a bit of self-confidence before most speakers are willing to move out from behind the lectern or podium. But if you are giving an extemporaneous speech, and you are familiar with the material, you should be able to move around a bit.

Your movement, from one place to another, provides action and gives the audience something to follow. It can help you engage your listeners as you walk around to the side or to the front on the lectern. In so doing, you have come out from behind the "barrier" and you become psychologically as well as physically closer to your listeners. Your movement can also help you emphasize a point. Move to a point "onstage," stop, pause verbally, look intently at your audience, and then make your statement with great emphasis in your voice. All these elements

—verbal and non-verbal—work together to emphasize your point, but it was the movement to a spot and then stopping and standing still, that initially got listeners' attention.

If you want to capture attention, change what you have been doing. Do the opposite. You have been standing still; then move. You have been moving; then stop and stand still.

Even positive things, if overdone, can become negatives. We have all seen the pacer—pacing back and forth continually like a caged animal. The constant movement soon becomes a distraction and interferes with the listeners' attention to and comprehension of the message. The key to the positive use of movement is to change. After moving a bit, stand still. When you have been standing still for a while, move again. In other words, once you have moved to a spot, plant yourself there for a while before moving again. Effective speakers know that judicious use of movement will help them capture and maintain listeners' attention as well as display their confidence. However, they also realize that overdoing movement makes them appear nervous and will be a distraction for the audience.

93. Use Natural Gestures to Generate Interest

Some individuals naturally use gestures with greater frequency than others. But most everyone does use gestures to some extent normally in everyday conversation. However, some people freeze and hold their bodies stiff in a public speaking situation. We have all observed the speaker who stands at the podium in a rigid stance—the toy soldier stance.

Gestures aid a speaker in several ways. The use of gestures help the speaker keep the attention of the audience and generate interest in his message. Certain gestures can help the speaker clarify the message as he outlines a shape, demonstrates the magnitude, or signals his exasperation with his hands.

Gestures can even be an aid to persuasion as the speaker adds emphasis or intensity of feeling with his gestures. Who can forget the picture of Nikita Khrushchev pounding his shoe on the podium as he spoke to the United Nations?

Besides the verbal messages that are complemented, clarified, or intensified by the use of appropriate gestures, an added benefit is that the speaker appears and actually feels more at ease with the use of gestures. The non-verbal message to the audience is one of competence and authority.

Let your natural use of gestures come through in your public speaking situations. If you view yourself on videotape and find you stand like a robot with few gestures and little movement, you can try to increase your movement as you practice. As you practice, purposely overdo your use of gestures. Gesture more frequently and with larger movements than feel comfortable. After you have practiced with this exaggerated use of movement for a while, then go back and practice a few times with what you feel is natural movement for you. Most people find their natural use of gestures will increase.

94. Talk With Your Listeners—Not At Them

Orators of yore spoke at people in a bombastic, elevated fashion. They most often talked at their listeners. Today's speakers, those who are both good and effective, talk **with** their listeners rather than **at** them. They see their audience and engage them as individuals. Their speeches don't sound memorized, nor do they sound as if they are read from manuscripts. The speaker conveys that he is sincere and truly concerned with each listener.

How does a speaker convey his concern and talk with his listeners? It is primarily conveyed through non-verbal behaviors. The speaker who talks **with** his listeners uses body language and paralanguage that says, "I care about this message. I care about you. This message is an important one for you." This is conveyed primarily through eye contact, through tone of voice, and through body language. The speaker doesn't just look out **at** the audience. The speaker makes eye contact that **locks** with the eyes of individual listeners and promotes a connection. The speaker's tone of voice is sincere rather than either flat or bombastic. The voice is projected and conveys confidence, but it is also sincere. He emphasizes points as he "punches" a word or phrase with his voice. There is feeling in his voice that comes across to the listeners.

The speaker doesn't stand stiffly behind a lectern. He moves occasionally, and if the setting is informal he will often come out from behind the lectern, thereby removing a barrier that otherwise stands between him and the audience. His body language is embracing rather than stiff and standoffish.

Listeners give greater credence to non-verbal messages than to verbal ones. We know people can say anything that may be conve-

> ▶ *Success Tip*

Pay particular attention to your non-verbal messages. Regardless of what you say, listeners give more credence to your non-verbal messages.

nient for them. But we believe it is more difficult to fake the messages that are conveyed non-verbally. Believe in what you speak about and allow that conviction to show in your delivery.

95. Hide Your "Errors"

One of the differences between a novice and a pro is that if the novice makes a blunder it is obvious to the entire audience. How? It is usually written all over the speaker's face—often with a terrified overdone grimace. This may be further emphasized with body language—the hunched movement of the shoulders coupled with the downward motion of the head—that says, "oops, I goofed." The speaker may also indicate with a verbal apology that he has committed an error.

The pro, on the other hand, realizes that if he just continues as if nothing unplanned has happened, most listeners will be blissfully unaware of whatever "mistake" has taken place. So his enthusiastic facial expression does not change except for whatever is appropriate to the message at the moment. His body language continues to say, "I am in control; what I have to say is important for you." Unless he has committed a verbal faux pas that must be rectified in order for the information to be correct, he will continue on as if nothing has happened out of the ordinary. If he misspoke and must correct himself, he will do it in a matter-of-fact way, keeping all his non-verbal cues professional and in control.

96. *Leave Playthings At Your Seat*

A nervous speaker will often play with anything he can get his hands on—and never be aware he is doing it. As we saw earlier, he may even distract his listeners by playing with the corners of the lectern! Since the speaker is not aware of what he is doing, it is best to leave things that could provide a distraction at one's seat or in one's briefcase.

The best rule is: don't take anything up to the front of the room unless you are using it for your presentation. In most cases your notes will be all you will use. Leave that pen at your seat, and you will not aimlessly take the cap on and off, or click the retractable point in and out, as you speak. Men, take those coins and keys out of your trouser's pocket before you speak, and you won't be constantly making jangling sounds as your nervous hands play with whatever is in your pocket. Women, refrain from wearing jangling jewelry that can be both an auditory and a visual distraction.

A word about two things you most likely will always have with you and cannot leave at your chair—your hands. Although they can be a real plus as your gestures complement your message and help maintain listener attention, your hands can also distract your listeners or focus their attention on the wrong things. Except for gestures, try to keep your hands at or below your waist. A speaker who continually pushes at a wisp of hair, frequently scratches his nose, or adjusts articles of clothing engages in hand motions that will distract the listener from concentrating on the message.

 **Caution!**

Don't take anything up to the front of the room unless you are using it for your presentation.

97. Use A Microphone Effectively, But Use It Sparingly

Why use a microphone sparingly? Because so many things can and do go wrong. It doesn't work properly; it cuts on and off; it squeals its ugly feedback at you and the audience; it either keeps you riveted behind the podium because it is stationary or the cord trips you as you try to move around with the older lavaliere microphones. So don't use a microphone just because it is there. Much of the equipment you are likely to encounter is antiquated or of questionable quality. Many speakers do not know how to use a microphone properly.

But if you find you will be speaking in a large auditorium or a room with poor acoustics, use a microphone, but use it effectively. The following guidelines should help you make effective use of a microphone. When you conducted your analysis of the situation you found out about the room where you would be speaking. So you should already know whether you will need to use a microphone. If so, you want to check the microphone ahead of when you present your speech—both to catch any problems with the particular mike as well as learn how to use **this** one. You may wish to check the mike and even practice using it several days prior to your presentation. Consider doing this for an especially important speech. When this is impractical, get to the event early enough so that you can check the microphone on the day of the speech before the audience is being seated. You want your listeners to first hear you when you actually begin your introduction.

Start by speaking into the mike—try about 4-6 inches away from the mike. Then try about 12 inches from the mike. Your best distance from the mike will probably be somewhere between these two points. You may find that at 10-12 inches from the mike it doesn't pick up your voice; you need to know where the mike cuts out. Don't just say a meaningless phrase such as, "testing, 1, 2, 3." That will not give you a test of your speaking volume when you speak with intensity as you will when you actually present your speech. Go through a bit of your speech (another reason you don't want the audience coming in as you check the mike) so that your actual speaking volume can be checked. Turn your head as if speaking to various members of the audience in different parts of the room. See whether the mike picks up equally well from these other angles. If possible, have someone sit near the back of the room and listen to whether you can be heard clearly.

If you are using a mike, you still need to project your voice. Part of your energy, part of your credibility comes from the dynamism that projection provides to your delivery. Don't give this up and speak softly because you think the microphone will carry your voice. So project your voice as you will in your speech, as you practice using the microphone.

Know how to raise and lower the mike if this applies to the microphone you will be using. You don't want to fumble with it as you begin your speech—remember that first impression! And it adds nothing to your credibility if you have to lean over or stand on your tiptoes throughout your speech! Know how to turn the mike on and off, and if it creates problems and becomes a distraction, turn it off. Turn your head if you have to cough; try not to cough into the mike. And it goes without saying, don't say anything near a microphone you wouldn't want everyone to hear. We can all remember noted people who have been embarrassed to find that some private comment has just been broadcast.

Learn to project your voice rather than use a microphone as a crutch, and if you do not need the microphone, don't use it. If the situation warrants the use of a microphone, hopefully you will have a state-of-the-art, voice-activated, cordless remote unit that will enhance rather than detract from your presentation. Use it effectively.

Respond To Your Audience

ANY YEARS AGO, AS PART OF AN ASSIGNMENT
for a graduate class in rhetorical criticism, I selected a
series of speeches delivered by Dr. Martin Luther
King, Jr. to analyze. The Canadian Broadcasting Corporation
sponsored The Massey Lectures annually and selected a noted
speaker to present the series each year. Dr. King had been the
speaker the previous year. The CBC made recordings of the
speeches available to me. As I listened to the first four speeches,
the delivery was the familiar one of Dr. King. But when I
listened to the fifth and final recording, my initial reaction was
that someone must have put the wrong recording in the jacket.
It did not sound at all like Dr. King's dynamic delivery. It was
flat; it was dull; it was lifeless.

A few days later I talked with Judith Somerville of the CBC
and mentioned to her how very different the delivery was for
the fifth of Dr. King's speeches. "That's interesting," she said.
"When the first four speeches were taped, Dr. King had a live

audience. For the fifth speech there was no live audience. The final speech was taped in a sound studio with only a microphone and a technician present." Dr. King was used to talking to live audiences. He responded to their feedback. Their responses energized his delivery! The audience will energize you as well if you establish that eye contact, connect with them, and let them connect with you.

98. Communicate Your Enthusiasm As Well As Your Ideas: Use Audience Feedback

Connect with your listeners. Not only will you engage them, but they will energize your delivery as well! If you are speaking to a group of listeners you do not know, try to arrive at the event early. Talk to a few people, if you can, before the program begins. This way you will have a few friendly faces to look at as you start your presentation. As you continue your speech, try to connect with other members of the audience. Eye contact is much more than looking up from one's notes and looking out at the audience. It is an attempt to connect with your listeners and engage them with you and your message.

Remember, they are not saber-toothed tigers sitting there. Don't be afraid to meet their gaze. You give to them your enthusiasm and they will give energy back to you. As you speak, you will probably identify a few people who are particularly expressive. They engage in a lot of positive non-verbal feedback. They smile, they nod their heads in agreement—behaviors that make you feel good. Communicate with them and use their positive responses to re-energize you. Look beyond these expressive people and try to engage additional members of your audience by connecting to their gaze and sharing your enthusiasm with them. Most will respond and you will have widened your pool of responsive listeners. If you feel your energy wane, go back and connect again with a listener who is part of your first group of friendly faces.

In every audience there will be a few people who seem unresponsive. They sit with little or no expression on their faces. These are the faces that strike terror into the hearts of all but the boldest speakers. Why? Because we tend to view a lack of expression as a negative expression. We look at that listener with the expressionless face and assume that he is bored or uninterested. However, after the speech the person with little expression may be the one who comes up to tell you how much he enjoyed your speech. So try not to let the lack of expression from some listeners get you down. Try to engage that person, then look back at one of your friendly faces to buoy you up again!

And In Conclusion . . .

99. Keep A File of Stories and Quotations

Some of those speakers that you envy so much have a secret—
they keep a file of stories or quotations that they think they
might be able to use sometime in a speech. Every time they hear
or read something they might be able to use, they write it down
or clip it out and put it in their file. They scan through the file
from time to time so that they remain familiar with what it
contains. When they need a great way to begin or end a speech
or an example as support for one of their main points, they can
go to their file.

How do they know what stories they will need for speeches
they may give in the future? They don't. But they can anticipate many of the topics they may be asked to present. You can
anticipate, too. And if you save a clipping you never use, no

harm is done. It is always better to have too much material rather than too little.

100. Seek & Accept Opportunities To Speak

Nervous about getting up to speak to an audience, many people avoid speaking situations whenever possible or decline invitations to present a speech. This only perpetuates the fear and doesn't give one the opportunity to grow as a speaker. The two things that will be most helpful to a speaker who wishes to combat nervousness are, first, to be thoroughly prepared for each speech one presents (Secret #1) and, second, to gain the experience of giving many speeches. With each successive, successful presentation the speaker gains experience and confidence.

So seek opportunities and accept invitations to speak. Each speaking situation is an opportunity for you to grow as a speech maker. As you gain experience, you will gain confidence and you will better be able to handle yourself in front of an audience.

101. Practice Makes Perfect— An Adage Gone Wrong

You have all heard the adage, "Practice makes perfect." Like so many things, if we hear it often enough, we tend to believe it. But in this case, the adage is wrong! The truth is, "Practice makes permanent." Practice tends to reinforce a behavior, but practice by itself does not correct inappropriate behaviors. To judge whether we are reinforcing good or bad behaviors, it is useful to have honest feedback from people with expertise in the area being judged.

You may enroll in a public speaking class or seminar to review the basics, polish your speaking skills, and receive useful criticism. But chances are you will need to continue to present speeches over a period of several weeks or months in order to gain the experience and confidence that will help you lessen the symptoms of nervousness—those darned butterflies or the wobbly knees.

Consider joining one of the many Toastmasters groups that are in communities across the country. Toastmasters, which is comprised of both men and women, provides a non-threatening opportunity to gain experience presenting speeches, and you will receive feedback from members as well. You can locate the Toastmasters groups in your area by checking their website at *www.toastmasters.org* or call 1-800-993-7732.

Practice these 101 secrets and you can construct a good speech as well as formulate an effective speech. Sharpen your delivery and present your speech with dynamism and you can be a successful, effective speaker. Develop your speaking skills and you develop the **power** to communicate your ideas and your enthusiasm to promote yourself, your business, and your passions. You will achieve the **power** to:

- stand up at your city council meeting and clearly state your views on the rezoning proposal the members will vote on later that evening.

- get behind the microphone at a PTA meeting and protest the school board's plan to close your child's school.

- accept that promotion, even though with the pay increase will come an increasing number of speaking assignments.

- present your company's reorganization plan persuasively to the stockholders.

You can achieve the **power** to present your ideas clearly, dynamically and convincingly whatever the situation. This is real **power**. This is the **power** of an **effective speaker** and this **power** is yours to develop and use.

Daniel Webster once said, "If all my talents and powers were to be taken from me by some inscrutable Providence, and I had my choice of keeping but one, I would unhesitatingly ask to be allowed to keep the power of speaking, for through it I would quickly recover all the rest." General H. Norman Schwartzkopf did not become a household name solely because of his talent as a military strategist. His military skills may give him a place in history books, but it was his effective presentation skills that gave him a place in the homes and hearts of America.

Appendix

9 Secrets to Command Attention

➤ Dress in a professional manner

➤ Walk to the lectern with a demeanor of confidence

➤ Stand erect behind the lectern

➤ Look at the audience and pause before you start to speak

➤ Project your voice to speak with authority

➤ Convey dynamism

➤ Begin with a powerful introduction

➤ Establish your credibility early

➤ Conclude; then leave the lectern with a confident, purposeful gait

10 Secrets to Control Fear

➤ You can never prepare too much

➤ Be totally familiar with your introduction

➤ Practice out loud and practice often

➤ Practice mentally

➤ Record your speech

➤ Concentrate on your message—not on yourself

➤ Know that to feel nervous is to be human

➤ Breathe deeply

➤ Channel your adrenaline into positive energy

➤ Know that you appear more confident than you feel

11 Secrets to Build Credibility

➤ Dress to convey authority and professionalism

➤ Project your voice

➤ Stand erect behind the lectern

➤ Use quotations or testimonies

➤ Offer statistics

➤ Use examples

➤ Compare or contrast ideas

➤ Demonstrate a concept

➤ Use visuals

➤ Restate ideas in a variety of ways

➤ Deliver the message dynamically

10 Secrets to Prepare Like a Pro

➤ Check out the speaking environment prior to your presentation

➤ Change the environment, if necessary, to fit your style

➤ Use the "3-Minute Prep" for unexpected speeches

➤ Use sheets of paper for notes—not note cards

➤ Use primarily nouns as notes to jog your memory

➤ Time your speech and edit, edit, edit

➤ Select a title that's a hit

➤ Prepare your "introducer" with an introduction

➤ Anticipate questions from the audience

➤ Have questions ready

8 Secrets to Close With Power

➤ Summarize your main points

➤ Refer to the occasion

➤ End with a powerful quotation

➤ Make a startling statement

➤ Leave listeners with a vivid illustration

➤ Issue a challenge or an appeal

➤ Keep a second closing in reserve

➤ Leave the lectern with a confident, purposeful gait

10 Secrets to Sharpen Your Delivery

➤ Speak clearly

➤ Vary your pace

➤ Use silent pauses often

➤ Limit use of vocalized pauses

➤ Vary your inflection

➤ Look at everyone frequently

➤ Use movement to maintain attention

➤ Use natural gestures to generate interest

➤ Hide your errors

➤ Leave playthings at your seat

Index

Author

CARYL RAE KRANNICH, PH.D., HAS OVER 30 YEARS experience teaching and conducting seminars in public speaking. She received her M.A. in Speech Communication from the University of Hawaii and her Ph.D. in Speech Communication from The Pennsylvania State University. As a university professor, management trainer, and consultant, she has trained thousands of individuals in the art of public speaking, from college students to government officials and corporate executives. She also has served as a speech writer for a cabinet official abroad. Her work has changed the lives and careers of many individuals who have dramatically improved their briefing and public speaking skills under Caryl's direction.

Caryl also is one of America's leading career and travel specialists with more than 45 books to her credit. She is the author of such best selling communication books as *Interview For Success* and *101 Dynamite Answers to Interview Questions*. Her international interests include consulting work in Asia and a unique global travel-shopping series, *The Treasures and Pleasures . . . Best of the Best in Travel and Shopping*. When not found at her home and business in Northern Virginia, she is somewhere in the world with her husband, Ron, working on their latest travel guide.

Caryl is Vice President of Development Concepts Incorporated, a training, consulting, and publishing firm in the Washington DC Metro area. Available for consultation and training, she can be contacted at <u>krannich@impactpublications.com</u>.

Connect To the Net

for all your career and travel resource needs!